97 Things Every Java Programmer Should Know

Collective Wisdom from the Experts

Kevlin Henney and Trisha Gee

Beijing · Boston · Farnham · Sebastopol · Tokyo

97 Things Every Java Programmer Should Know

by Kevlin Henney and Trisha Gee

Published by O'Reilly Media, Inc., 1005 Gravenstein Highway North, Sebastopol, CA 95472.

O'Reilly books may be purchased for educational, business, or sales promotional use. Online editions are also available for most titles (*http://oreilly.com*). For more information, contact our corporate/institutional sales department: 800-998-9938 or *corporate@oreilly.com*.

Acquisitions Editor: Suzanne McQuade	**Indexer:** Ellen Troutman-Zaig
Developmental Editor: Corbin Collins	**Interior Designer:** David Futato
Production Editor: Beth Kelly	**Cover Designer:** Karen Montgomery
Copyeditor: Piper Editorial	**Illustrator:** Rebecca Demarest
Proofreader: Sonia Saruba	

June 2020:   First Edition

Revision History for the First Edition

2020-05-15:   First Release

See *http://oreilly.com/catalog/errata.csp?isbn=9781491952696* for release details.

978-1-491-95269-6

[LSI]

To the memory of those who shaped us
through their wisdom and compassion

Table of Contents

Preface

The mind is not a vessel that needs filling, but wood that needs igniting.
—Plutarch

What should every Java programmer know? It depends. It depends on who you ask, why you ask, and when you ask. There are at least as many suggestions as there are points of view. In a language, platform, ecosystem, and community that affects the software and lives of so many people, and has done so from one century to the next, from one core to many, from megabytes to gigabytes, it depends on more than you could ever hope to cover in a single book by a single author.

Instead, in this book, we draw on some of those many perspectives to collect together for you a cross section and representation of the thinking in the Java-verse. It's not *every* thing, but it is 97 of them from 73 contributors. To quote the preface of *97 Things Every Programmer Should Know* (O'Reilly):

> With so much to know, so much to do, and so many ways of doing so, no single person or single source can lay claim to "the one true way." The contributions do not dovetail like modular parts, and there is no intent that they should—if anything, the opposite is true. The value of each contribution comes from its distinctiveness. The value of the collection lies in how the contributions complement, confirm, and even contradict one another. There is no overarching narrative: it is for you to respond to, reflect on, and connect together what you read, weighing it against your own context, knowledge, and experience.

What should every Java programmer know? In the 97 things we have sampled, the answers span the language, the JVM, testing techniques, the JDK, community, history, agile thinking, implementation know-how, professionalism, style, substance, programming paradigms, programmers as people, software architecture, skills beyond code, tooling, GC mechanics, non-Java JVM languages…and more.

Permissions

In the spirit of the first *97 Things* books, each contribution in this volume follows a nonrestrictive, open source model. Each contribution is licensed under a Creative Commons Attribution 4.0 license (*https://oreil.ly/zPsKK*). Many of the contributions also first appeared in the *97 Things* Medium publication (*https://medium.com/97-things*).

All these things are fuel and fire for your thoughts and your code.

O'Reilly Online Learning

 For more than 40 years, *O'Reilly Media* has provided technology and business training, knowledge, and insight to help companies succeed.

Our unique network of experts and innovators share their knowledge and expertise through books, articles, and our online learning platform. O'Reilly's online learning platform gives you on-demand access to live training courses, in-depth learning paths, interactive coding environments, and a vast collection of text and video from O'Reilly and 200+ other publishers. For more information, visit *http://oreilly.com*.

How to Contact Us

Please address comments and questions concerning this book to the publisher:

O'Reilly Media, Inc.
1005 Gravenstein Highway North
Sebastopol, CA 95472
800-998-9938 (in the United States or Canada)
707-829-0515 (international or local)
707-829-0104 (fax)

We have a web page for this book, where we list errata, examples, and any additional information. You can access this page at *https://oreil.ly/97Tejpsk*.

Email *bookquestions@oreilly.com* to comment or ask technical questions about this book.

Visit *http://oreilly.com* for news and information about our books and courses.

Find us on Facebook: *http://facebook.com/oreilly*.

Follow us on Twitter at *http://twitter.com/oreillymedia*, and also check out *http://twitter.com/97_Things*.

Watch us on YouTube: *http://youtube.com/oreillymedia*.

Acknowledgments

Many people have contributed their time and their insight, both directly and indirectly, to the *97 Things Every Java Programmer Should Know* project. They all deserve credit.

We would like to thank all those who took the time and effort to contribute to this book. We are also grateful for the additional feedback, comments, and suggestions provided by Brian Goetz.

Thanks to O'Reilly for the support they have provided for this project, including Zan McQuade and Corbin Collins for their guidance and for nurturing contributors and content, and Rachel Roumeliotis, Susan Conant, and Mike Loukides for their contributions on this journey.

Kevlin would also like to thank his wife, Carolyn, for making sense of his nonsense, and his sons, Stefan and Yannick, for making sense of their parents.

Trisha would like to add thanks to her husband, Isra, for helping her to see that stressing about not doing enough was not helping her to do anything, and her daughters, Evie and Amy, for providing unconditional love and cuddles.

We hope this book will be informative, insightful, and inspirational.

Enjoy!

All You Need Is Java

Anders Norås

While working on the first major revision of Visual Studio, the team at Microsoft introduced the world to three developer personas: Mort, Elvis, and Einstein.

Mort was the opportunistic developer, doing quick fixes and making things up as he went along. Elvis was the pragmatic programmer, building solutions for the ages while learning on the job. Einstein was the paranoid programmer, obsessed with designing the most efficient solution and figuring everything out before writing his code.

On the Java side of the religious divide of programming languages, we laughed at Morts, and we wanted to be Einsteins building frameworks to make sure the Elvises wrote their code the "right way."

This was the dawn of the age of the frameworks, and unless you were proficient with the latest, greatest object relational mapper and inversion of control framework, you weren't a proper Java programmer. Libraries grew into frameworks with prescripted architectures. And as these frameworks became technology ecosystems, many of us forgot about the little language that could—Java.

Java is a great language and its class library has something for every occasion. Need to work with files? `java.nio`'s got you covered. Databases? `java.sql` is the place to go. Almost every Java distribution even sports a full-blown HTTP server, even if you have to climb off the Java-named branch and onto `com.sun.net.httpserver`.

As our applications move toward serverless architectures, where the deployment units can be single functions, the benefits we get from application frameworks diminish. This is because we'll likely spend less time on handling technical and infrastructural concerns, focusing our programming efforts toward the business capabilities our programs realize.

As Bruce Joyce put it:

> We have to reinvent the wheel every once in a while, not because we need a
> lot of wheels; but because we need a lot of inventors.

Many have set out to build generic business logic frameworks to maximize reuse. Most have failed since there really aren't any generic business problems. Doing something special in a specific way is what sets one business apart from the next. This is why you're guaranteed to be writing business logic on just about every project. In the name of coming up with something generic and reusable, one might be tempted to introduce a rules engine or similar. At the end of the day, configuring a rules engine is programming, often in a language inferior to Java. Why not try to just write Java instead? You'll be surprised to find that the end result will be easy to read, which in turn makes the code easy to maintain—even by non-Java programmers.

Quite often you'll find that Java's class library is a little limited, and you might need something to make working with dates, networking, or something else a little more comfortable. That's fine. Use a library. The difference is that you'll now be using that library because a specific need occurred, not because it was part of the stack you've always been using.

The next time an idea for a small program springs to mind, awaken your knowledge of the Java class library from hibernation rather than reaching for that JHipster scaffold. Hipsterism is *passé*; living a simple life is where it's at now. I bet Mort loved the simple life.

Approval Testing

Emily Bache

Have you ever written a test assertion with a dummy or blank expectation? Something like this:

```
assertEquals("", functionCall())
```

Where `functionCall` is returning a string and you're not sure exactly what that string should be, but you'll know it's right when you see it? When you run the test the first time, of course, it fails because `functionCall` returns a string that isn't empty. (You might have several tries, until the return value looks correct.) Then you paste this value instead of the empty string in the `assertEquals`. Now the test should pass. Result! That's what I'd call *approval testing*.

The crucial step here is when you decide the output is correct and use it as the expected value. You "approve" a result—it's good enough to keep. I expect you've done this kind of thing without really thinking about it. Perhaps you call it by a different name: it's also called *snapshot testing* or *golden master testing*. In my experience, if you have a testing framework specifically designed to support it, then a lot of things fall into place and testing this way gets easier.

With a classic unit testing framework like JUnit, it can be a bit painful to update those expected strings when they change. You end up pasting stuff around in the source code. With an approval testing tool, the approved string gets stored in a file instead. That immediately opens up new possibilities. You can use a proper diff tool to go through changes and merge them one by one. You can get syntax highlighting for JSON strings and such. You can search and replace updates across several tests in different classes.

So, what are good situations for approval testing? Here are a few:

Code without unit tests that you need to change
> If the code is in production, then anything it does is, by default, considered correct and can be approved. The hard part about creating tests

turns into a problem of finding seams and carving out pieces of logic that return something interesting you can approve.

REST APIs and functions that return JSON or XML
If the result is a longer string, then storing it outside the source code is a big win. JSON and XML can both be formatted with consistent white space so they are easy to compare against an expected value. If there are values in the JSON or XML that vary a lot—dates and times, for example—you might need to check them separately before replacing them with a fixed string and approving the remainder.

Business logic that builds a complex return object
Start by writing a `Printer` class that can take your complex return object and format it as a string. Think of a `Receipt` or a `Prescription` or an `Order`. Any of those could be represented well as a human-readable multiline string. Your `Printer` can choose to only print a summary—traverse the object graph to pull out relevant details. Your tests will then exercise various business rules and use the Printer to create a string for approval. If you have a noncoding product owner or business analyst, they could even read the test results and verify that they are correct.

If you already have tests that make assertions about strings that are longer than one line, then I recommend finding out more about approval testing and starting to use a tool that supports it.

Augment Javadoc with AsciiDoc

James Elliott

Java developers already know Javadoc. Those who've been around a long time remember how transformative it was, as Java became the first mainstream language to integrate a documentation generator right into the compiler and standard toolchain. The resulting explosion of API documentation (even if not always great or polished) has hugely benefited us all, and the trend has spread to many other languages. As James Gosling reported (*https://oreil.ly/Y_7rk*), Javadoc was initially controversial because "a good tech writer could do a lot better job"—but there are vastly more APIs than tech writers to document them, and the value of having something universally available has been well established.

Sometimes you need more than API documentation, though—much more than you can fit in the package and project overview pages Javadoc offers. End-user-focused guides and walk-throughs, detailed background on architecture and theory, explanations of how to fit together multiple components...none of these fit comfortably within Javadoc.

So what can we use to meet these other needs? The answers have changed over time. FrameMaker was a groundbreaking cross-platform GUI technical document powerhouse in the '80s. Javadoc even used to include a MIF Doclet for generating attractive printed API documentation with Frame-Maker—but only a vestigial Windows version remains. DocBook XML offers similar structural and linking power, with an open specification and cross-platform toolchain, but its raw XML format is impractical to work with directly. Keeping up with its editing tools became expensive and tedious, and even the good ones felt clunky and hampered the flow of writing.

I'm thrilled to have found a better answer: AsciiDoc (*https://oreil.ly/NYrJI*) offers all the power of DocBook in an easy-to-write (and read) text format, where doing simple things is trivial and doing complex things is possible. Most AsciiDoc constructs are as immediately readable and accessible as other lightweight markup formats like Markdown, which are becoming familiar through online discussion forums. And when you need to get fancy, you can include complex equations using MathML or LaTeX formats, formatted source code listings with numbered and linked callouts to text paragraphs, admonition blocks of different kinds, and more.

AsciiDoc was introduced with a Python implementation in 2002. The current official implementation (and steward of the language) is Asciidoctor (*https://oreil.ly/aRRvG*), released in 2013. Its Ruby code can also be run in the JVM through AsciidoctorJ (*https://oreil.ly/UT8EP*) (with Maven and Gradle plug-ins) or transpiled to JavaScript (*https://oreil.ly/E_6qn*), all of which work nicely in continuous integration environments. When you need to build an entire site of related documentation (even from multiple repositories), tools like Antora (*https://antora.org*) make it shockingly easy. The community (*https://oreil.ly/PtWwa*) is friendly and supportive, and watching its growth and progress over the past year has been inspiring. And, if it matters to you, the process of standardizing a formal AsciiDoc specification is underway (*https://oreil.ly/BaXa8*).

I like creating rich, attractive documentation (*https://oreil.ly/H_rSW*) for the projects that I share. AsciiDoc has made that so much easier, and given me such rapid turnaround cycles, that polishing and perfecting that documentation has become fun (*https://oreil.ly/7sbtj*). I hope you find the same. And, coming full circle, if you decide to go all in with AsciiDoc, there's even a Doclet (*https://oreil.ly/9KgQq*) named Asciidoclet that lets you write Javadoc using AsciiDoc!

Be Aware of Your Container Surroundings

David Delabassee

There is a danger to containerizing legacy Java applications as is, with their legacy Java Virtual Machine (JVM), because the ergonomics of those older JVMs will be fooled when running inside Docker containers.

Containers have become the de facto runtime packaging mechanism. They provide many benefits: a certain level of isolation, improved resource utilization, the ability to deploy applications across different environments, and more. Containers also help reduce the coupling between an application and the underlying platform, as that application can be packaged into a portable container. This technique is sometimes used to modernize legacy applications. In the case of Java, a container embeds a legacy Java application along with its dependencies, including an older version of the JVM used by that application.

The practice of containerizing legacy Java applications with their environments can certainly help keep older applications running on modern, supported infrastructure by decoupling them from older, unsupported infrastructure. But the potential benefits of such a practice come with their own set of risks due to the JVM ergonomics.

JVM ergonomics (*https://oreil.ly/h3hTh*) enables the JVM to tune itself by looking at two key environmental metrics: the number of CPUs and the available memory. With these metrics, the JVM determines important parameters such as which garbage collector to use, how to configure it, the heap size, the size of the ForkJoinPool, and so on.

Linux Docker container support, added in JDK 8 update 191 (*https://oreil.ly/ C_1AW*), allows the JVM to rely on Linux cgroups (*https://oreil.ly/nDIwb*) to get the metrics of resources allocated to the container it runs in. Any JVM older than that is not aware that it is running within a container and will access metrics from the host OS and not from the container itself. And, given that in most cases a container is configured to only use a subset of the host resources, the JVM will rely on incorrect metrics to tune itself. This quickly leads to an unstable situation in which the container will likely get killed by the host as it tries to consume more resources than are available.

The following command shows which JVM parameters are configured by the JVM ergonomics:

```
java -XX:+PrintFlagsFinal -version | grep ergonomic
```

JVM container support is enabled by default but can be disabled by using the -XX:-UseContainerSupport JVM flag. Using this JVM flag in a container with restricted resources (CPU and memory) allows you to observe and explore the impact of JVM ergonomics with and without container support.

Running legacy JVMs in Docker containers is clearly not recommended. But if that is the only option, the legacy JVM should at least be configured to not exceed the resources allocated to the container it runs in. The ideal, obvious solution is to use a modern, supported JVM (for example, JDK 11 or later) that will not only be container-aware by default but will also provide an up-to-date and secure runtime.

Behavior Is "Easy"; State Is Hard

Edson Yanaga

When I was first introduced to object-oriented programming, some of the very first concepts taught were the triple of polymorphism, inheritance, and encapsulation. And to be honest, we spent quite some time trying to understand and code with them. But, at least for me, too much emphasis was given to the first two, and very little to the third and most important of all: encapsulation.

Encapsulation allows us to tame the growing state and complexity that is a constant in the software development field. The idea that we can internalize the state, hide it from other components, and offer only a carefully designed API surface for any state mutation is core to the design and coding of complex information systems.

But, at least in the Java world, we have failed to spread some of the best practices about the construction of well-encapsulated systems. JavaBean properties on anemic classes that simply expose internal state through *getters* and *setters* are common, and with Java Enterprise architectures we seem to have popularized the concept that most—if not all—business logic should be implemented in service classes. Within them we use getters to extract the information, process them to get a result, and then put the result back into our objects with setters.

And when the bugs bite, we dig through log files, use debuggers, and try to figure out what's happening with our code in production. It's fairly "easy" to spot bugs caused by behavior issues: pieces of code doing something they're not supposed to do. On the other hand, when our code seems to be doing the right thing and we still have bugs, it becomes much more complicated. From my experience, the hardest bugs to solve are the ones caused by *inconsistent state*. You've reached a state in your system that shouldn't happen, but there it is—a NullPointerException for a property that was never supposed to be null, a negative value that should only be positive, and so on.

The odds of finding the steps that led to such an inconsistent state are low. Our classes have surfaces that are too mutable and too easily accessed: any piece of code, anywhere in the system, can mutate our state without any kind of checks or balances.

We sanitize user-provided inputs through validation frameworks, but that "innocent" setter is still there allowing any piece of code to call it. And I won't even discuss the likelihood of someone using UPDATE statements directly on the database to change some columns in database-mapped entities.

How can we solve this problem? *Immutability* is one of the possible answers. If we can guarantee that our objects are immutable, and the state consistency is checked on object creation, we'll never have an inconsistent state in our system. But we have to take into account that most Java frameworks do not cope very well with immutability, so we should at least aim to minimize mutability. Having properly coded factory methods and builders can also help us to achieve this minimally mutable state.

Therefore, don't generate your setters automatically. Take time to think about them. Do you really need that setter in your code? And if you decide that you do, perhaps because of some framework requirement, consider using an *anti-corruption layer* to protect and validate your internal state after those setter interactions.

Benchmarking Is Hard— JMH Helps

Michael Hunger

Benchmarking on the JVM, especially microbenchmarking, is hard. It's not enough to throw a nanosecond measurement around a call or loop and be done. You have to take into account warm-up, HotSpot compilation, code optimizations like inlining and dead code elimination, multithreading, consistency of measurement, and more.

Fortunately, Aleksey Shipilëv, the author of many great JVM tools, contributed JMH, the Java Microbenchmarking Harness (*https://oreil.ly/gR0fd*), to the OpenJDK. It consists of a small library and a build system plug-in. The library provides annotations and utilities to declare your benchmarks as annotated Java classes and methods, including a BlackHole class to consume generated values to avoid code elimination. The library also offers correct state handling in the presence of multithreading.

The build system plug-in generates a JAR with the relevant infrastructure code for running and measuring the tests correctly. That includes dedicated warm-up phases, proper multithreading, running multiple forks and averaging across them, and much more.

The tool also outputs important advice on how to use the gathered data and limitations thereof. Here is an example for measuring the impact of presizing collections:

```
public class MyBenchmark {
    static final int COUNT = 10000;
    @Benchmark
    public List<Boolean> testFillEmptyList() {
        List<Boolean> list = new ArrayList<>();
        for (int i=0;i<COUNT;i++) {
            list.add(Boolean.TRUE);
        }
```

```
        return list;
    }
    @Benchmark
    public List<Boolean> testFillAllocatedList() {
        List<Boolean> list = new ArrayList<>(COUNT);
        for (int i=0;i<COUNT;i++) {
            list.add(Boolean.TRUE);
        }
        return list;
    }
}
```

To generate the project and run it, you can use the JMH Maven archetype:

```
mvn archetype:generate \
-DarchetypeGroupId=org.openjdk.jmh \
-DarchetypeArtifactId=jmh-java-benchmark-archetype \
-DinteractiveMode=false -DgroupId=com.example \
-DartifactId=coll-test -Dversion=1.0


cd coll-test


# add com/example/MyBenchmark.java


mvn clean install


java -jar target/benchmarks.jar -w 1 -r 1


...
# JMH version: 1.21
...
# Warmup: 5 iterations, 1 s each
# Measurement: 5 iterations, 1 s each
# Timeout: 10 min per iteration
# Threads: 1 thread, will synchronize iterations
# Benchmark mode: Throughput, ops/time
# Benchmark: com.example.MyBenchmark.testFillEmptyList


...


Result "com.example.MyBenchmark.testFillEmptyList":
  30966.686 ±(99.9%) 2636.125 ops/s [Average]
```

```
(min, avg, max) = (18885.422, 30966.686, 35612.643), stdev = 3519.152
CI (99.9%): [28330.561, 33602.811] (assumes normal distribution)

# Run complete. Total time: 00:01:45

REMEMBER: The numbers below are just data. To gain reusable insights,
you need to follow up on
why the numbers are the way they are. Use profilers (see -prof,
-lprof), design factorial
experiments, perform baseline and negative tests that provide
experimental control, make sure
the benchmarking environment is safe on JVM/OS/HW level, ask for
reviews from the domain experts.
Do not assume the numbers tell you what you want them to tell.
Benchmark                            Mode  Cnt    Score     Error   Units
MyBenchmark.testFillAllocatedList thrpt 25  56786.708 ± 1609.633  ops/s
MyBenchmark.testFillEmptyList        thrpt 25  30966.686 ± 2636.125  ops/s
```

So we see that our preallocated collection is almost twice as fast as the default instance because it doesn't have to be resized during the addition of elements.

JMH is a powerful tool in your toolbox to write correct microbenchmarks. If you run them in the same environment, they are even comparable, which should be the main way of interpreting their results. They can also be used for profiling purposes, as they provide stable, repeatable results. Aleksey (*https://oreil.ly/5zWU1*) has much more to say about the topic if you're interested.

The Benefits of Codifying and Asserting Architectural Quality

Daniel Bryant

Your continuous delivery build pipeline should be the primary location where agreed-upon architectural qualities for your applications are codified and enforced. However, these automated quality assertions shouldn't replace continued team discussions about standards and quality levels, and they should definitely not be used to avoid intra- or inter-team communication. That said, checking and publishing quality metrics within the build pipeline can prevent the gradual decay of architectural quality that might otherwise be hard to notice.

If you're wondering why you should test your architecture, the ArchUnit motivation page (*https://oreil.ly/q1OCY*) has you covered. It starts with a familiar story: once upon a time, an architect drew a series of nice architectural diagrams that illustrated the components of the system and how they should interact. Then the project got bigger and use cases more complex, new developers dropped in and old developers dropped out. This eventually led to new features being added in any way that fit. Before long, everything depended on everything, and any change could have an unforeseeable effect on any other component. I'm sure many readers will recognize this scenario.

ArchUnit (*https://www.archunit.org*) is an open source, extensible library for checking the architecture of your Java code by using a Java unit-test framework like JUnit or TestNG. ArchUnit can check for cyclic dependencies and check dependencies between packages and classes, and layers and slices, and more. It does all this by analyzing Java bytecode and importing all classes for analysis.

To use ArchUnit in combination with JUnit 4, include the following dependency from Maven Central:

```
<dependency>
    <groupId>com.tngtech.archunit</groupId>
    <artifactId>archunit-junit</artifactId>
    <version>0.5.0</version>
    <scope>test</scope>
</dependency>
```

At its core, ArchUnit provides infrastructure to import Java bytecode into Java code structures. You can do this using `ClassFileImporter`. You can make architectural rules such as "services should be accessed only by controllers" by using a DSL-like fluent API, which can in turn be evaluated against imported classes:

```
import static com.tngtech.archunit.lang.syntax.ArchRuleDefinition;
// ...
@Test
public void Services_should_only_be_accessed_by_Controllers() {
    JavaClasses classes =
        new ClassFileImporter().importPackages("com.mycompany.myapp");
    ArchRule myRule = ArchRuleDefinition.classes()
        .that().resideInAPackage("..service..")
        .should().onlyBeAccessed()
        .byAnyPackage("..controller..", "..service..");
    myRule.check(classes);
}
```

Extending the preceding example, you can also enforce more layer-based access rules using this test:

```
@ArchTest
public static final ArchRule layer_dependencies_are_respected =
layeredArchitecture()
.layer("Controllers").definedBy("com.tngtech.archunit.eg.controller..")
.layer("Services").definedBy("com.tngtech.archunit.eg.service..")
.layer("Persistence").definedBy("com.tngtech.archunit.eg.persistence..")
.whereLayer("Controllers").mayNotBeAccessedByAnyLayer()
.whereLayer("Services").mayOnlyBeAccessedByLayers("Controllers")
.whereLayer("Persistence").mayOnlyBeAccessedByLayers("Services");
```

You can also ensure that naming conventions such as class name prefixes are followed, or specify that a class named a certain way must be in an appropriate package. GitHub contains a host of ArchUnit examples (*https:// oreil.ly/Xv8CI*) to get you started and give you ideas.

You could attempt to detect and fix all of the architectural issues mentioned here by having an experienced developer or architect look at the code once a week, identify violations, and correct them. However, humans are notorious for not acting consistently and, when the inevitable time pressures are placed on a project, often the first thing to be sacrificed is manual verification.

A more practical method is to codify the agreed-upon architectural guidelines and rules using automated tests, using ArchUnit or another tool, and include them as part of your continuous integration build. Any issues can then be quickly detected and fixed by the engineer who caused the issue.

Break Problems and Tasks into Small Chunks

Jeanne Boyarsky

You're learning to program. You receive a small assignment. You write under a thousand lines of code. You type it in and test. Then you add print statements or use a debugger. Maybe you get coffee. Then you puzzle over what you were thinking.

Sound familiar? And that's just a toy problem. Work tasks and systems are far larger. Big problems take time to solve. And worse, there is too much to hold in your brain's RAM.

A good way to deal with this is to break the problem into small chunks. The smaller the better. If you can get that one small piece working, then you don't have to think about it anymore and can move on to the next piece. When doing this well, you want to write automated tests for each small problem. You should also commit frequently. That gives you a rollback point when things don't work as expected.

I remember helping out a teammate who was stuck. I asked when he had last committed, because the easiest fix would be to roll back and reapply the change. The answer was "a week ago." Then he had two problems: the original one and that I wouldn't help him debug a week's worth of work.

After that experience, I ran a training session for my team on how to break tasks into smaller chunks. I was told by the senior developers that their tasks were "special" and "couldn't possibly be broken up." When you hear the word *special* in relation to a task, you should immediately be suspicious.

I decided to schedule a second meeting. Everyone was responsible for bringing an example of a "special" task, and I would help them break it up. The first example was a screen that was scheduled to take two weeks to develop. I split it up like this:

- Create a *hello world* screen at the right URL—no fields, just prints *hello world*.
- Add functionality to display a list from a database.
- Add a text area.
- Add a select pull-down.
- *<A long list of more tiny tasks>*

And guess what? After each of these tiny tasks, there could be a commit. This means commits could happen many times a day.

Then I was told that this could be done for screens, but file processing was "special." Now what did I say about the word *special*? I split that up as well:

- Read a line from the file.
- Validate the first field, including the database call.
- Validate the second field and transform it using business logic.
- *<A bunch of fields later>*
- Apply the first business logic rule to all fields.
- *<A bunch of rules later>*
- Add a message to the queue.

Again, the task wasn't special. If you think a task is special, pause and think about why. Often you will find this technique still applies.

Finally, a developer told me he couldn't commit his code in any less than a week. The task wound up being reassigned to me. I did some extra committing to make a point. Counting, I committed 22 times in the 2 days it took to me complete the task. Maybe if he'd committed more frequently, it would have been done faster!

Build Diverse Teams

Ixchel Ruiz

Years ago, a good doctor knew it all, did it all: set a fracture, performed surgery, drew blood. A good doctor was independent and self-sufficient, and autonomy was highly valued.

Fast forward to today. Knowledge has exploded, surpassing the individual and bringing about specialization. In order to provide an adequate solution from beginning to end, many specialists will be involved, and different teams will have to interact.

This is true in software development as well.

Cooperation is now one of the highest-valued traits in "good" professionals. In the past, independence and self-sufficiency was enough to be "good." Now we all need to behave like pit crews: team members.

The challenge is to build teams that are both successful and diverse.

Four types of diversity—industry background, country of origin, career path, and gender—positively correlate with innovation. In a homogenous team, regardless of academic background, there may be redundant perspectives. Women, for example, bring disruptive innovation.

How big is the impact? In management teams with a high gender diversity, an increase of 8% in revenue from innovation has been observed.

Differences among group members can also be a source of insight—members with different backgrounds, experiences, and ideas increase the pool of information, skills, and networks. With more perspectives, reaching consensus requires constructive debate. If the environment where ideas are exchanged is positive, creative solutions will emerge naturally.

But increasing group diversity is not an easy task. Conflict can arise when heterogeneous groups don't communicate effectively or divide themselves into factions. People prefer to collaborate with those similar to them. A close-knit group will develop its own language and culture, and outsiders will be distrusted. Distance, along with the pitfalls of mishaps in digital communication, make software teams especially prone to the problems of "us versus them" and incomplete information.

So how do we get the benefits of diversity and avoid the drawbacks?

The key in collaboration is developing psychological safety and trust within your team.

When we are surrounded with people we can trust, even if they are different from us, we're more confident to take risks and experiment. When we trust each other, we can look to others to provide information or perspective that will help solve a challenging problem, thus creating opportunities for cooperation. We can overcome vulnerable situations when feedback is requested.

In teams with psychological safety, it's easier for people to believe that the benefits of speaking up outweigh the costs. Participation leads to less resistance to change, and the more frequently people participate, the more likely they are to offer novel ideas.

Personality matters in software development, too; it's equally important to build an environment of trust for different personalities. We all have a colleague who is willing to test every new library, framework, or tool, someone thinking how to use or explore the new shiny red toy, sometimes with surprising results. Some are inclined to establish new processes, code format styles, or templates for commit messages, and will remind us when we are not following proper procedure. You may have teammates who will under-promise and overdeliver, and ones who are thinking of everything that can go wrong: updating dependencies, installing patches, security risks, etc. Consider everyone's differences, and don't push too hard.

We can increase diversity in our teams in two dimensions: background and personality. If we have good team dynamics and continue to build trust in each other, we will be more successful as programmers.

Builds Don't Have To Be Slow and Unreliable

Jenn Strater

A while back, I was working at an early-stage start-up where the codebase and development team were growing every day. As we added more and more tests, the builds were taking longer and longer to run. At around the eight-minute mark I started to notice it, which is why I remember that specific number. From eight minutes, build times nearly doubled. At first, it was kinda nice. I would kick off a build, go grab a coffee, and chat with coworkers on other teams. But after a few months, it became irritating. I'd had enough coffee and I knew what everyone was working on, so I would check Twitter or help other developers on my team while waiting for my builds to finish. I would then have to context switch when I went back to my work.

The build was also unreliable. As is normal for any software project, we had a number of flaky tests. The first, albeit naive, solution was to turn off the tests (i.e., @Ignore) that were failing. Eventually, it got to the point where it was easier to push the changes and rely on the continuous integration (CI) server than to run the tests locally. The problem with this tactic was that it moved the problem further down the line. If a test failed at the CI step, it took much longer to debug. And if a flaky test passed initially and only showed up after merging, it blocked the entire team until we determined whether it was a legitimate issue.

Frustrated, I tried to fix some of the problematic tests. One test in particular stands out in my mind. It only appeared when the entire test suite ran, so each time I made a change, I had to wait 15-plus minutes for feedback. These incredibly long feedback cycles and a general lack of relevant data meant I wasted days tracking down this bug.

This isn't just about one company, though. One of the advantages of being a job hopper is that I've seen the way many different teams work. I thought these issues were normal until I started at a company where we work on exactly these problems.

Teams that follow Developer Productivity Engineering, the practice and philosophy of improving developer experience through data, are able to improve their slow and unreliable builds. These teams are happier and have higher throughput, making the business happier too.

No matter what build tool they are using, the people responsible for developer productivity can effectively measure build performance and track outliers and regressions for both local and CI builds. They spend time analyzing the results and finding bottlenecks in the build process. When something does go wrong, they share the reports (e.g., Gradle build scans) with teammates and compare failing and passing builds to pinpoint the exact problem—even if they can't reproduce the issues on their own machines.

With all this data, they can actually do something to optimize the process and reduce the frustration developers are facing. This work is never done, so they keep iterating to maintain developer productivity. It's not an easy task, but the teams who work at it are able to prevent the problems I described from happening in the first place.

"But It Works on My Machine!"

Benjamin Muschko

Have you ever joined a new team or project and had to try to find your way around the infrastructure needed to build the source code on your developer's machine? You're not alone, and you may have had questions:

- What JDK version and distribution are required to compile the code?
- What if I'm running Linux, but everyone else is on Windows?
- What IDE do you use, and which version do I need?
- What version of Maven or other build tool do I need to install to properly run through developer workflows?

I hope the answer you got to these questions wasn't "Let me have a look at the tools installed on my machine"—every project should have a clearly defined set of tools that are compatible with the technical requirements to compile, test, execute, and package the code. If you're lucky, these requirements are documented in a playbook or wiki, although as we all know, documentation easily becomes outdated, and keeping the instructions in sync with the latest changes takes concerted effort.

There's a better way to solve the problem. In the spirit of *infrastructure as code*, tooling providers came up with the *wrapper*, a solution that helps with provisioning a standardized version of the build tool runtime without manual intervention. It *wraps* the instructions required to download and install the runtime. In the Java space, you'll find the Gradle Wrapper (*https://oreil.ly/CmZP1*) and the Maven Wrapper (*https://oreil.ly/xu50T*). Even other tooling, like Bazel, Google's open source build tool, provides a launching mechanism (*https://oreil.ly/OY7R7*).

Let's see how the Maven Wrapper works in practice. You have to have the Maven runtime installed on your machine to generate the so-called Wrapper files. Wrapper files represent the scripts, configuration, and instructions every developer of the project uses to build the project with a predefined version of the Maven runtime. Consequently, those files should be checked into SCM alongside the project source code for further distribution.

The following runs the Wrapper goal provided by the Takari Maven plug-in (*https://oreil.ly/sI2pO*):

```
mvn -N io.takari:maven:0.7.6:wrapper
```

The following directory structure shows a typical Maven project augmented by the Wrapper files, marked in bold:

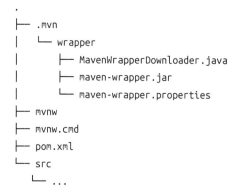

```
.
├── .mvn
│   └── wrapper
│       ├── MavenWrapperDownloader.java
│       ├── maven-wrapper.jar
│       └── maven-wrapper.properties
├── mvnw
├── mvnw.cmd
├── pom.xml
└── src
    └── ...
```

With the Wrapper files in place, building the project on any machine is straightforward: run your desired goal with the *mvnw* script. The script automatically ensures the Maven runtime will be installed with the predefined version set in *maven-wrapper.properties*. Of course, the installation process is only invoked if the runtime isn't already available on the system.

The following command execution uses the script to run the goals *clean* and *install* on a Linux, Unix, or macOS system:

```
./mvnw clean install
```

On Windows, use the batch script ending with the file extension *.cmd*:

```
mvnw.cmd clean install
```

What about running typical tasks in the IDE or from your CI/CD pipeline? You'll find other execution environments derive the same runtime configuration from the Wrapper definition as well. You just have to ensure the Wrapper scripts are called to invoke the build.

Gone are the days of "But it works on my machine!"—standardize once, build everywhere! Introduce the wrapper concept to any JVM project to improve build reproducibility and maintainability.

The Case Against Fat JARs

Daniel Bryant

In modern Java web development, the thought of packaging and running applications in anything other than a fat JAR is almost becoming heretical. However, there can be distinct disadvantages to building and deploying these artifacts. One obvious issue is the typically large size of fat JARs, which can consume excess storage space and network bandwidth. In addition, the monolithic build process can take a long time and cause developers to context switch while waiting. The lack of shared dependencies can also cause inconsistency across the use of utilities, such as logging, and challenges with integration of communication or serialization across services.

The use of fat JARs for deploying Java applications became popular alongside the rise of the microservice architecture style, DevOps, and cloud-native technologies, such as public cloud, containers, and orchestration platforms. As applications were being decomposed into a collection of smaller services that were being run and managed independently, it made sense from an operational perspective to bundle all of the application code into a single executable binary. A single artifact is easier to keep track of, and the standalone execution removes the need to run additional application servers. However, some organizations are now bucking the trend and creating "skinny JARs."

The HubSpot engineering team has discussed how the challenges listed above were impacting their development life cycle in a blog post, "The Fault in Our JARs: Why We Stopped Building Fat JARs" (*https://oreil.ly/WqX2D*). They ultimately created a new Maven plug-in: SlimFast (*https://oreil.ly/ 3Kf5Y*). This plug-in differs from the classic Maven Shade plug-in that the majority of Java developers are familiar with, in that it separates the application code from the associated dependencies and accordingly builds and uploads two separate artifacts. It may sound inefficient to build and upload the application dependencies separately, but this step occurs only if the dependencies have changed. With many applications the dependencies change infrequently, and so this step is often a no-op; the package dependencies' JAR file is uploaded to remote storage only a minimal number of times.

The SlimFast plug-in uses the Maven JAR plug-in to add a `Class-Path` manifest entry to the skinny JAR that points to the dependencies' JAR file, and generates a JSON file with information about all the dependency artifacts in S3 so that these can be downloaded later. At deploy time, the build downloads all of the application's dependencies, but then caches these artifacts on each of the application servers, so this step is usually a no-op as well. The net result is that at build time, only the application's skinny JAR is uploaded to the remote storage, which is typically only a few hundred kilobytes. At deploy time, only this same thin JAR needs to be downloaded to the target deployment environment, which takes a fraction of a second.

One of the core ideas behind the emergence of DevOps is that the development and operations team (and all the other teams) should work together for a common goal. The choice of deployment artifact format is an important decision within the goal of being able to continuously deploy functionality to end users. Everyone should collaborate in order to understand the requirements in relation to how this impacts the developer experience and ability to manage resources involved in deploying.

The SlimFast plug-in is currently tied to AWS S3 for the storage of artifacts, but the code is available on GitHub, and the principles can be adapted for any type of external storage.

The Code Restorer

Abraham Marin-Perez

Always remember, the person we're really working for is the person who's restoring the piece a hundred years from now. He's the one we want to impress.

That quote is from Hobie, a character in Donna Tartt's novel *The Goldfinch*. Hobie is an antique furniture restorer. I am particularly thankful for this quote because it beautifully expresses what I've always thought about code: the best code is written thinking about the programmers that come after.

I think current software practices suffer from an illness caused by too much haste. Much like trees in a crowded jungle, the aim is to outgrow the competition. Trees competing for light often overstretch themselves, growing tall and thin and becoming susceptible to small disturbances. Strong winds or mild disease can make them collapse. I'm not saying we don't need to look at short-term benefits—in fact, I encourage it—just not at the expense of long-term stability.

Today's software industry is like these trees. Many "modern" teams focus only on the next week or month. Companies struggle just to live another day, another sprint, another cycle. And nobody seems to worry about this. Developers can always find another job, and so can managers. Entrepreneurs can try and cash out before the company has lost its value. So can the VC that backed the initial investment. Too often, the key to success lies in timing the exit so as to leave just before people realize that the amazing growth was just a tumor.

On the other hand, maybe that's not so bad. Some pieces of furniture are meant to last hundreds of years, and some will likely crumble within a decade. You can spend thousands at Sotheby's on a china cabinet—or go to IKEA and probably furnish your whole house. Maybe we just need to understand this new economy we've created, where everything is ephemeral and transient. Assets aren't expected to last long, just long *enough*. We aren't supposed to create things that stand the test of time, just the test of *profit*.

And yet I believe there is a middle point, a new role beginning to take form: the code restorer. Doing something that lasts forever at the first go is so expensive that it isn't worth it, but focusing only on short-term profit will create code that collapses under its own weight. This is where the code restorer comes in, somebody whose job isn't to "recreate the same thing but better" (a common wish that almost always fails), but rather to take the existing codebase and slowly reshape it to make it manageable again. Add some tests here, break down that ugly class there, remove unused functionality, and give it back improved.

We, as programmers, have to decide what kind of software we want to build. We can focus on profit for a while, build up something that holds, but at some point we have to choose between durability, carefully reshaping the code, or profit, abandoning it and starting afresh. After all, profits are essential, but some things are bigger than money.

Concurrency on the JVM

Mario Fusco

Originally, raw threads were the only concurrency model available on the JVM, and they're still the default choice for writing parallel and concurrent programs in Java. When Java was designed 25 years ago, however, the hardware was dramatically different. The demand for running parallel applications was lower, and the concurrency advantages were limited by the lack of multicore processors—tasks could be decoupled, but not executed simultaneously.

Nowadays, the availability and expectation of parallelization has made the limitations of explicit multithreading clear. Threads and locks are too low-level: using them correctly is hard; understanding the Java Memory Model even harder. Threads that communicate through shared mutable state are unfit for massive parallelism, leading to nondeterministic surprises when access isn't properly synchronized. Moreover, even if your locks are arranged correctly, the purpose of a lock is to restrict threads running in parallel, thus reducing the degree of parallelism of your application.

Because Java does not support distributed memory, it's impossible to scale multithreaded programs horizontally across multiple machines. And if writing multithreaded programs is difficult, testing them thoroughly is nearly impossible—they frequently become a maintenance nightmare.

The simplest way to overcome the shared memory limitations is to coordinate threads via distributed queues instead of locks. Here, message passing replaces shared memory, which also improves decoupling. Queues are good for unidirectional communication but may introduce latency.

Akka makes the actor model, popularized by Erlang, available on the JVM, and is more familiar to Scala programmers. Each actor is an object responsible for manipulating only its own state. Concurrency is implemented with message flow between actors, so they can be seen as a more structured way of using queues. Actors can be organized in hierarchies, providing for built-in fault tolerance and recovery through supervision. Actors also have some drawbacks: untyped messages don't play well with Java's current lack of pattern matching, message immutability is necessary but cannot currently be enforced in Java, composition can be awkward, and deadlocking between actors is still possible.

Clojure takes a different approach with its built-in software transactional memory, turning the JVM heap into a transactional data set. Like a regular database, data is modified with (optimistic) transactional semantics. A transaction is automatically retried when it runs into some conflict. This has the advantage of being nonblocking, eliminating many problems associated with explicit synchronization. This makes them easy to compose. Additionally, many developers are familiar with transactions. Unfortunately, this approach is inefficient in massively parallel systems where concurrent writes are more likely. In these situations retries are increasingly costly and performance can become unpredictable.

Java 8 lambdas promote the use of functional programming properties in code, such as immutability and referential transparency. While the actor model reduces the consequences of mutable state by preventing sharing, functional programming makes the state shareable because it prohibits mutability. Parallelizing code made of pure, side-effect-free functions can be trivial, but a functional program can be less time efficient than its imperative equivalent and may place a bigger burden on the garbage collector. Lambdas also facilitate the use of the reactive programming paradigm in Java consisting in asynchronous processing of streams of events.

There is no silver bullet for concurrency, but there are many different options with different trade-offs. Your duty as a programmer is to know them and choose the one that best fits the problem at hand.

CountDownLatch—Friend or Foe?

Alexey Soshin

Let's imagine a situation in which we'd like to launch multiple concurrent tasks, and then wait on their completion before proceeding further. The ExecutorService makes the first part easy:

```
ExecutorService pool = Executors.newFixedThreadPool(8);
Future<?> future = pool.submit(() -> {
    // Your task here
});
```

But how do we wait for all of them to complete? CountDownLatch comes to our rescue. A CountDownLatch takes the number of invocations as a constructor argument. Each task then holds a reference to it, calling the count Down method when the task completes:

```
int tasks = 16;
CountDownLatch latch = new CountDownLatch(tasks);
for (int i = 0; i < tasks; i++) {
    Future<?> future = pool.submit(() -> {
        try {
            // Your task here
        }
        finally {
            latch.countDown();
        }
    });
}
if (!latch.await(2, TimeUnit.SECONDS)) {
    // Handle timeout
}
```

This example code will launch 16 tasks, then wait for them to finish before proceeding further. There are some important points to take note of, though:

1. Make sure that you release the latch in a `finally` block. Otherwise, if an exception occurs, your main thread may wait forever.

2. Use the `await` method that accepts a timeout period. That way, even if you forget about the first point, your thread will wake up sooner or later.

3. Check the return value of the method. It returns `false` if the time has elapsed, or `true` if all the tasks managed to complete on time.

As mentioned earlier, `CountDownLatch` receives its count on creation. It can be neither increased nor reset. If you're looking for capabilities that are similar to those of `CountDownLatch` but with the ability to reset the count, you should check out `CyclicBarrier` instead.

`CountDownLatch` is useful in many different situations. It becomes especially useful when you're testing your concurrent code, since it allows you to make sure that all the tasks are complete before checking their results.

Consider the following real-world example. You have a proxy and an embedded server, and you'd like to test that when the proxy is called, it invokes the correct endpoint on your server.

Obviously, it doesn't make much sense to issue a request before both the proxy and server have started. One solution is to pass a `CountDownLatch` to both methods, and continue with the test only when both parties are ready:

```
CountDownLatch latch = new CountDownLatch(2);
Server server = startServer(latch);
Proxy proxy = startProxy(latch);
boolean timedOut = !latch.await(1, TimeUnit.SECONDS);
assertFalse(timedOut, "Timeout reached");
// Continue with test if assertion passes
```

You just need to make sure that both the `startServer` and `startProxy` methods call `latch.countDown` once they have successfully started.

`CountDownLatch` is very useful, but there's one important catch: you shouldn't use it in production code that makes use of concurrent libraries or frameworks, such as Kotlin's coroutines, Vert.x, or Spring WebFlux. This is because `CountDownLatch` blocks the current thread. Different concurrency models don't play well together.

Declarative Expression Is the Path to Parallelism

Russel Winder

In the beginning, Java was an imperative, object-based programming language. Indeed, it still is. Over the years, though, Java has evolved, at each stage becoming more and more a language of declarative expression. *Imperative* is all about the code explicitly telling the computer what to do. *Declarative* is about the code expressing a goal abstracting over the way in which the goal is achieved. Abstraction is at the heart of programming, and so the move from imperative code to declarative code is a natural one.

At the core of declarative expression is the use of higher-order functions, functions that take functions as parameters and/or return functions. This was not an integral part of Java originally, but with Java 8 it moved front and center: Java 8 was a turning point in the evolution of Java, allowing replacement of imperative expression with declarative expression.

An example—trivial but nonetheless indicative of the main issue—is to write a function that returns a List containing the squares of the argument List to the function. Imperatively, we might write:

```
List<Integer> squareImperative(final List<Integer> datum) {
  var result = new ArrayList<Integer>();
  for (var i = 0; i < datum.size(); i++) {
    result.add(i, datum.get(i) * datum.get(i));
  }
  return result;
}
```

The function creates an abstraction over some low-level code, hiding the details from the code that uses it.

With Java 8 and beyond, we can use streams and express the algorithm in a more declarative way:

```
List<Integer> squareDeclarative(final List<Integer> datum) {
  return datum.stream()
              .map(i -> i * i)
              .collect(Collectors.toList());
}
```

This sets out at a higher level of expression of *what* is to be done; the details of *how* are left to the library implementation. Classic abstraction. True, the implementation is within a function that already abstracts and hides, but which would you rather maintain: the low-level imperative implementation or the high-level declarative implementation?

Why is this such a big deal? The above is a classic example of an embarrassingly parallel computation. The evaluation of each result depends only on one item of input; there is no coupling. So we can write:

```
List<Integer> squareDeclarative(final List<Integer> datum) {
  return datum.parallelStream()
              .map(i -> i * i)
              .collect(Collectors.toList());
}
```

Doing so, we will get the maximum parallelism that the library is able to extract from the platform. Because we are abstracting away from the details of how, focusing only on the goal, we can turn a sequential data-parallel computation into a parallel one trivially.

It will be left as an exercise for the reader to (attempt to) write a parallel version of the imperative code should they so wish. Why? Because for data parallel problems, using Streams is the right abstraction. To do anything else is to deny the Java 8 evolution of Java.

Deliver Better Software, Faster

Burk Hufnagel

For me, *Deliver Better Software, Faster* is a guiding principle, and one I strongly recommend you adopt because it describes what must happen to keep your users happy. In addition (and perhaps more importantly), following it can result in a more enjoyable and interesting career. To see how, let's examine the three parts of this important idea:

1. *Deliver* means taking responsibility for more than just writing and debugging code. Despite appearances, you aren't paid to write code. You're paid to make it easier for your users to do something they find valuable, and until your code is running in production, they won't benefit from your hard work.

   Changing your focus from writing code to delivering software requires understanding the overall process for getting your changes into production and then doing two key things:

   - Making sure you *aren't* doing things that hinder the process, like guessing the meaning of a vague requirement instead of asking for clarification before implementing it.

   - Making sure you *are* doing things that speed up the process, like writing and running automated tests to show your code meets the acceptance criteria.

2. *Better Software* is shorthand for two ideas you should already be familiar with: "building the right thing" and "building the thing right." The first means ensuring that what you've written meets all the requirements and acceptance criteria. The second is about writing code that is easily understood by another programmer so they can successfully fix bugs or add new features.

While this may sound easy to do, especially if you follow a practice like test-driven development (TDD), many teams tend to lean one way or the other:

- Nonprogrammers might push developers to take shortcuts to deliver new features sooner, with promises to come back and "do it right" later.

- Sometimes programmers who just learned something will try to use it everywhere possible, even if they know a simpler solution would work just as well.

In either case, the balance is lost and the resulting technical debt increases the time needed to deliver value to your users until the balance is regained.

3. *Faster* refers to both *Deliver* and *Better Software*, and could be a challenging goal because people trying to do complicated things quickly tend to make mistakes. To me, the obvious solution includes:

   - Using a process like TDD to create automated tests, then regularly running the automated unit, integration, and user acceptance tests to verify the system's behavior.

   - Building and running an automated process that runs all the tests in multiple environments and, assuming they all pass, deploys the code to production.

Both of these processes will be done multiple times and require great attention to detail—just the sort of task a computer does faster and more accurately than a person. That's good because I have one more recommendation: deploy changes to production more often so each deployment has fewer changes and is therefore less likely to have problems, and your users get the benefits of your work sooner.

Adopting *Deliver Better Software, Faster* as a guiding principle is both challenging and fun. Be aware that it will take time to find and fix all the places that need work, but the rewards are worth it.

Do You Know What Time It Is?

Christin Gorman

At what time does the Scandinavian Airlines plane from Oslo to Athens arrive on Monday? Why are questions that seem so easy in day-to-day life so difficult in programming? Time should be simple, just seconds passing, something a computer is very good at measuring:

```
System.currentTimeMillis() = 1570964561568
```

Although correct, 1570964561568 is not what we want when we ask what time it is. We prefer 1:15 p.m., October 13, 2019.

It turns out that time is two separate things. On the one hand, we have seconds passing. On the other, we have an unhappy marriage between astronomy and politics. Answering the question "What time is it?" depends on the location of the sun in the sky relative to your position along with the political decisions made in that region up to that point in time.

Many of the problems we have with date and time in code come from mixing these two concepts. Using the latest `java.time` library (or Noda Time (*https://nodatime.org*) in .NET) will help you. Here are three main concepts to help you reason correctly about time: `LocalDateTime`, `ZonedDateTime`, and `Instant`.

`LocalDateTime` refers to the concept 1:15 p.m., October 13, 2019. There can be any number of these on the timeline. `Instant` refers to a specific point on the timeline. It is the same in Boston as in Beijing. To get from a `LocalDate Time` to an `Instant`, we need a `TimeZone`, which comes with Coordinated Universal Time (UTC) offsets and daylight saving time (DST) rules at the time. `ZonedDateTime` is a `LocalDateTime` with a `TimeZone`.

Which ones do you use? There are so many pitfalls. Let me show you a few. Let's say we're writing software to organize an international conference. Will this work?

```java
public class PresentationEvent {
  final Instant start, end;
  final String title;
}
```

Nope.

Although we need to represent a particular point in time, for future events, even when we know the time and the time zone, we cannot know the instant ahead of time because DST rules or UTC offsets might change between now and then. We need a `ZonedDateTime`.

How about regularly occurring events, like a flight? Will this work?

```java
public class Flight {
  final String flightReference;
  final ZonedDateTime departure, arrival;
}
```

Nope.

This can fail twice a year. Imagine a flight leaving Saturday at 10:00 p.m. and arriving Sunday at 6:00 a.m. What happens when we move the clock back an hour because of daylight savings? Unless the aircraft circles uselessly during the extra hour, it's going to land at 5:00 a.m., not 6:00 a.m. When we move ahead one hour, it'll arrive at 4:00 a.m. For recurring events with duration, we cannot fix both the start and the end. Here's what we need:

```java
public class Flight {
  final String flightReference
  final ZonedDateTime departure;
  final Duration duration;
}
```

What about events that start at 2:30 a.m.? Which one? There may be two, or it might not exist at all. In Java, the following methods handle the autumnal DST transition:

```java
ZonedDateTime.withEarlierOffsetAtOverlap()
ZonedDateTime.withLaterOffsetAtOverlap()
```

In Noda Time, specify both DST transitions explicitly with `Resolvers`.

I have only scratched the surface of potential issues, but as they say, good tools are half the work. Use `java.time` (or Noda Time), and you've saved yourself a lot of errors.

Don't hIDE Your Tools

Gail Ollis

What is the one essential tool every Java programmer needs? Eclipse? IntelliJ IDEA? NetBeans? No. It's *javac*. Without it, all you have is files of weird-looking text. It is possible to do the job without integrated development environments (IDEs)—ask people like me who programmed in the olden days. It is not possible to program without essential development tools.

Given that they are central to the task, it's surprising how rarely people use tools like *javac* directly. While knowing how to make effective use of an IDE is important, understanding what it is doing, and how, is crucial.

Once upon a time, I worked on a project with two subsystems, one in C++ and the other in Java. C++ programmers worked with their editor of choice and the command line. Java programmers used an IDE. One day, the incantation to interact with the version control system changed. It was a simple command-line change for the C++ programmers, who went on their way without delay. The Java team spent the whole morning wrestling with their Eclipse configuration. They finally got back to productive work in the afternoon.

This unfortunate story doesn't reflect well on the Java team's mastery of their chosen tools. But it also illustrates how distanced they were in their day-to-day work from the *essential* tools of their trade by working exclusively in an IDE. Information hiding is a great principle for enabling focus on a useful abstraction rather than a mass of detail, for sure. But it implies a *choice* to delve into details only when relevant, not ignorance of the details.

Relying solely on an IDE can undermine a programmer's mastery of their tools because the IDE purposely hides the nuts and bolts. The configuration —often just a case of following someone else's instructions—can be forgotten as soon as it's done. There are many advantages to also knowing how to use the essential tools directly:

- "It works on my machine" scenarios are less likely and simpler to resolve if you understand the relationships among tools, source code, other resources, and generated files. It also helps with knowing what to package for installation.

- It's extraordinarily quick and easy to set different options. Start with commands like `javac --help` so you can see what those options are.

- Familiarity with the essential tools is valuable when helping people who use a different environment. It also helps when something goes wrong; it's hard to troubleshoot when integrated tools are not working. Visibility is better on the command line and you can isolate parts of the process, just as you would when debugging code.

- You have access to a richer tool set. You can integrate any combination of tools that have a command-line interface (for example, scripts or Linux commands), not just those supported in the IDE.

- End users will not run your code in an IDE! In the interest of good user experience, test from the start by running the code as it will be run on a user's machine.

None of this denies the benefits of an IDE. But to be truly skilled at your craft, understand your essential tools and don't let them get rusty.

Don't Vary Your Variables

Steve Freeman

I try to make as many variables as possible `final` because I find it easier to reason about immutable code. It makes my coding life simpler, which is a high priority for me—I've spent too much time trying to figure out exactly how the contents of a variable change throughout a block of code. Of course, Java's support for immutability is more limited than some other languages, but there are still things we can do.

Assign Once

Here's a small example of a structure I see everywhere:

```
Thing thing;
if (nextToken == MakeIt) {
    thing = makeTheThing();
} else {
    thing = new SpecialThing(dependencies);
}
thing.doSomethingUseful();
```

To me this doesn't irrevocably express that we're going to set the value of `thing` before we use it and not change it again. It takes me time to walk through the code and figure out that it won't be `null`. It's also an accident waiting to happen when we need to add more conditions and don't quite get the logic right. Modern IDEs will warn about an unset `thing`—but then lots of programmers ignore warnings. A first fix would be to use a *conditional* expression:

```
final var thing = nextToken == MakeIt
                ? makeTheThing()
                : new SpecialThing(dependencies);
thing.doSomething();
```

The only way through this code is to assign `thing` a value.

A next step is to wrap up this behavior in a function to which I can give a descriptive name:

```
final var thing = aThingFor(nextToken);
thing.doSomethingUseful();

private Thing aThingFor(Token aToken) {
    return aToken == MakeIt
            ? makeTheThing()
            : new SpecialThing(dependencies);
}
```

Now the life cycle of thing is easy to see. Often this refactoring shows that thing is only used once, so I can remove the variable:

```
aThingFor(aToken).doSomethingUseful();
```

This approach sets us up for when, inevitably, the condition becomes more complicated; note that the switch statement is simpler without the need for repeated break clauses:

```
private Thing aThingFor(Token aToken) {
    switch (aToken) {
        case MakeIt:
            return makeTheThing();
        case Special:
            return new SpecialThing(dependencies);
        case Green:
            return mostRecentGreenThing();
        default:
            return Thing.DEFAULT;
    }
}
```

Localize Scope

Here's another variant:

```
var thing = Thing.DEFAULT;
// lots of code to figure out nextToken
if (nextToken == MakeIt) {
    thing = makeTheThing();
}
thing.doSomethingUseful();
```

This is worse because the assignments to `thing` aren't close together and might not even happen. Again, we extract this into a supporting method:

```
final var thing = theNextThingFrom(aStream);

private Thing theNextThingFrom(Stream aStream) {
    // lots of code to figure out nextToken
    if (nextToken == MakeIt) {
        return makeTheThing();
    }
    return Thing.DEFAULT;
}
```

Alternatively, separating concerns further:

```
final var thing = aThingForToken(nextTokenFrom(aStream));
```

Localizing the scope of anything that is variable into a supporting method makes the top-level code predictable. Finally, although some coders aren't used to it, we could try a streaming approach:

```
final var thing = nextTokenFrom(aStream)
                    .filter(t -> t == MakeIt)
                    .findFirst()
                    .map(t -> makeTheThing())
                    .orElse(Thing.DEFAULT);
```

I've regularly found that trying to lock down anything that does not vary makes me think more carefully about my design and flushes out potential bugs. It forces me to be clear about where things can change and to contain such behavior into local scopes.

Embrace SQL Thinking

Dean Wampler

Look at this query:

```
SELECT c.id, c.name, c.address, o.items FROM customers c
JOIN orders o
ON o.customer_id = c.id
GROUP BY c.id
```

We acquire all the customers who have orders, including their names and addresses, along with the details of their orders. Four lines of code. Anyone with a little SQL experience, including nonprogrammers, can understand this query.

Now think about a Java implementation. We might declare classes for Customer and Order. I remember well-meaning consultants saying we should also create classes to encapsulate collections of them, rather than use "naked" Java collections. We still need to query the database, so we pull in an object-relational mapper (ORM) tool and write code for that. Four lines of code quickly turn into dozens or even hundreds of lines. The few minutes it took to write and refine the SQL query stretch into hours or days of editing, writing unit tests, code reviews, and so on.

Can't we just implement the whole solution with only the SQL query? Are we *sure* we can't? Even if we really can't, can we eliminate waste and write only what's essential? Consider the qualities of the SQL query:

We don't need a new table for the join output, so we don't create one.
    The biggest failing of *applied* object-oriented programming has been the belief that you should faithfully reproduce your domain model in code. In reality, a few core type definitions are useful for encapsulation and understanding, but tuples, sets, arrays, and so forth are all we need the rest of the time. Unnecessary classes become a burden as the code evolves.

The query is declarative.

Nowhere does it tell the database how to *do* the query; it just states the *relational constraints* the database must satisfy. Java is an imperative language, so we tend to write code that says what to do. Instead, we should declare constraints and desired outcomes, and then isolate the *how* implementation in one place or delegate to a library that can implement it for us. Like functional programming, SQL is declarative. In functional programming, equivalent declarative implementations are achieved using composable primitives, such as *map*, *filter*, *reduce*, and so on.

The domain-specific language (DSL) is well matched to the problem.

DSLs can be somewhat controversial. It's very hard to design a good one, and the implementations can be messy. SQL is a data DSL. It's quirky, but its longevity is proof of how well it expresses typical data-processing needs.

All applications are really data applications. At the end of the day, everything we write is a data manipulation program, whether or not we think of it that way. Embrace that fact and the unnecessary boilerplate will reveal itself, allowing you to write only what's essential.

Events Between Java Components

A.Mahdy AbdelAziz

One of the core concepts of object orientation in Java is that every class can be considered to be a *component*. Components can be extended or included to form bigger components. The final application is also considered a component. Components are like Lego blocks that build up a bigger structure.

An event in Java is an action that changes the state of a component. For example, if your component is a button, then clicking on that button is an event that changes the state of the button to be *clicked*.

Events do not necessarily happen only on visual components. For example, you can have an event on a USB component that a *device is connected*. Or an event on a network component that *data is transferred*. Events help to decouple the dependencies between components.

Assume we have an Oven component and a Person component. These two components exist in parallel and work independently of one another. We should not make Person part of Oven, nor the other way around. To build a smart house, we want the Oven to prepare food once Person is hungry. Here are two possible implementations:

1. Oven checks Person in fixed, short intervals. This annoys Person and is also expensive for Oven if we want it to check on multiple instances of Person.

2. Person comes with a public event, Hungry, to which Oven is subscribed. Once Hungry is fired, Oven is notified and starts preparing food.

The second solution uses the event architecture to handle the listening and communication between components efficiently and without a direct coupling between Person and Oven, because Person will fire the event, and any component, such as `Oven`, `Fridge`, and `Table`, can listen to that event without any special handling from the `Person` component.

Implementing events for a Java component can take different forms, depending on how they are expected to be handled. To implement a minimal `Hunger Listener` in the `Person` component, first, create a listener interface:

```
@FunctionalInterface
public interface HungerListener {
    void hungry();
}
```

Then, in the `Person` class, define a list to store the listeners:

```
private List<HungerListener> listeners = new ArrayList<>();
```

Define an API to insert a new listener:

```
public void addHungerListener(HungerListener listener) {
    listeners.add(listener);
}
```

You can create a similar API for removing a listener. Also, add a method to trigger the action of being hungry to notify all listeners of the event:

```
public void becomesHungry() {
    for (HungerListener listener : listeners)
        listener.hungry();
}
```

Finally, from the `Oven` class, add code that listens to the event and implements the action when the event is fired:

```
Person person = new Person();
person.addHungerListener(() -> {
    System.err.println("The person is hungry!");
    // Oven takes action here
});
```

And to try it out:

```
person.becomesHungry();
```

For fully decoupled code, the last section should be in an independent class that has an instance of `Person` and `Oven`, and handles the logic between them. Similarly, we can add other actions for `Fridge`, `Table`, and so on. They all will get notified only once the `Person` `becomesHungry`.

Feedback Loops

Liz Keogh

- Because our product managers don't know what they want, they find out from the customers. They sometimes get this wrong.

- Because our product managers don't know everything about systems, they invite other experts to become stakeholders in the project. The stakeholders get it wrong.

- Because I don't know what to code, I find out from our product managers. We sometimes get this wrong.

- Because I make mistakes while writing code, I work with an IDE. My IDE corrects me when I'm wrong.

- Because I make mistakes in understanding the existing code, I use a statically typed language. The compiler corrects me when I'm wrong.

- Because I make mistakes while thinking, I work with a pair. My pair corrects me when I'm wrong.

- Because my pair is human and also makes mistakes, we write unit tests. Our unit tests correct us when we're wrong.

- Because we have a team that is also coding, we integrate with their code. Our code won't compile if we're wrong.

- Because our team makes mistakes, we write acceptance tests that exercise the whole system. Our acceptance tests will fail if we're wrong.

- Because we make mistakes writing acceptance tests, we get three amigos together to talk through them. Our amigos will tell us if we're wrong.

- Because we forget to run the acceptance tests, we get our build to run them for us. Our build will tell us if we're wrong.

- Because we didn't think of every scenario, we get testers to explore the system. Testers will tell us if it's wrong.

- Because we only made it work on Henry's laptop, we deploy the system to a realistic environment. The tests will tell us if it's wrong.

- Because we sometimes misunderstand our product manager and other stakeholders, we showcase the system. Our stakeholders will tell us if we're wrong.

- Because our product manager sometimes misunderstands the people that want the system, we put the system in production. The people who want it tell us if we're wrong.

- Because people notice things going wrong more than things going right, we don't just rely on opinions. We use analytics and data. The data will tell us if we're wrong.

- Because the market keeps changing, even if we were right before, eventually we'll be wrong.

- Because it costs money to get it wrong, we do all these things as often as we can. That way we are only ever a little bit wrong.

- Don't worry about getting it right. Worry about how you'll know it's wrong, and how easy it will be to fix when you find out. Because it's probably wrong.

- It's OK to be wrong.

Firing on All Engines

Michael Hunger

Traditional Java profilers use either byte code instrumentation or sampling (taking stack traces at short intervals) to determine where time was spent. Both approaches add their own skews and oddities. Understanding the output of those profilers is an art of its own and requires quite some experience.

Fortunately, Brendan Gregg (*https://oreil.ly/dhd5O*), a performance engineer at Netflix, came up with *flame graphs* (*https://oreil.ly/2kCDd*), an ingenious kind of diagram for stack traces that can be gathered from almost any system.

A flame graph sorts and aggregates the traces up to each stack level, so that their count per level represents the percentage of the total time spent in that part of the code. Rendering those blocks as actual blocks (rectangles) with the width being proportional to the percentage and stacking the blocks onto each other turned out to be very useful.

The "flames" represent from bottom to top the progression from the entry point of the program or thread (main or an event loop) to the leaves of the execution in the tips of the flames. Note that the left-to-right order has no significance; often, it's just alphabetical sorting. The same is true for colors. Only the relative widths and stack depths are relevant.

You can immediately see if certain parts of the program take an unexpectedly large amount of time. The higher up in the diagram that happens, the worse it is. Especially if you have a flame that's very wide on top, you know you've found a bottleneck that is not delegating work elsewhere. After fixing the issue, measure again, and if the overall performance issue persists, revisit the diagram for new indications.

To address the shortcomings of traditional profilers, many modern tools make use of an internal JVM feature (AsyncGetCallTrace) that allows the gathering of stack traces outside of safepoints. Additionally, they combine measurement of JVM operations with native code and system calls to the operating system so that time spent in network, input/output (I/O), or garbage collection can become part of the flame graph as well.

Tools like Honest Profiler, perf-map-agent, async-profiler, and even IntelliJ IDEA make capturing the information and generating flame graphs really easy.

In most cases, you just download the tool, provide the process ID (PID) of your Java process, and tell the tool to run for a certain amount of time and generate the interactive scalable vector graphics (SVG):

```
# download and unzip async profiler for your OS from:
# https://github.com/jvm-profiling-tools/async-profiler
./profiler.sh -d <duration> -f flamegraph.svg -s -o svg <pid> && \
open flamegraph.svg  -a "Google Chrome"
```

The SVG that the tools produce is not just colorful but also interactive. You can zoom into sections, search for symbols, and more.

Flame graphs are an impressively powerful tool to quickly get an overview of the performance characteristics of your programs; you can see hotspots immediately and focus on those. Including non-JVM aspects also helps with the bigger picture.

Follow the Boring Standards

Adam Bien

At the beginning of the Java age, there were dozens of incompatible application servers on the market, and the server vendors followed completely different paradigms. Some servers were even partially implemented in native languages like C++. Understanding multiple servers was hard, and porting an application from one server to another was nearly impossible.

APIs like JDBC (introduced with JDK 1.1), JNDI (introduced with JDK 1.3), JMS, JPA, or Servlets abstracted, simplified, and unified already established products. EJBs and CDI made the deployment and programming models vendor agnostic. J2EE, later Java EE and now Jakarta EE, and MicroProfile defined a minimal set of APIs an application server had to implement. With the advent of J2EE, a developer only had to know a set of J2EE APIs to develop and deploy an application.

Although the servers evolved, the J2EE and Java EE APIs remained compatible. You never had to migrate your application to run on a newer release of the application server. Even upgrading to a higher Java EE version was painless. You only had to re-test the application without even recompiling it. Only if you wanted to take advantage of newer APIs did you have to refactor the application. With the introduction of J2EE, developers could master multiple application servers without delving too deep into their specifics.

We have a very similar situation in the web/JavaScript ecosystem right now. Frameworks like jQuery, Backbone.js, AngularJS 1, Angular 2+ (completely different from AngularJS 1), ReactJS, Polymer, Vue.js, and Ember.js follow completely different conventions and paradigms. It has become hard to master multiple frameworks at the same time. The initial goal of many frameworks was to address incompatibility issues among different browsers. As browsers became surprisingly compatible, frameworks started to support data binding, unidirectional data flow, and even enterprise Java features like dependency injection.

At the same time, browsers became not only more compatible but also provided features previously available only with third-party frameworks. The function `querySelector` is available in all browsers and provides comparable functionality to jQuery's DOM access capabilities. Web Components with Custom Elements, Shadow DOM, and Templates enable developers to define new elements containing UI and behavior, and even to structure entire applications. As of ECMAScript 6, JavaScript became more similar to Java, and ES6 modules made bundling optional. The MDN (Mozilla Developer's Framework) became a unified effort from Google, Microsoft, Mozilla, W3C, and Samsung to provide a home for web standards.

Now it's possible also to build frontends without frameworks. Browsers have an excellent track record for being backward compatible. All the frameworks have to use the browser APIs regardless, so by learning the standards you also understand the frameworks better. As long as browsers don't introduce any breaking changes, just relying on web standards without any frameworks is enough to make your application last.

Focusing on standards allows you to gain knowledge incrementally over time —an efficient way to learn. Evaluating popular frameworks is exciting, but the gained knowledge isn't necessarily applicable to the next "hot thing."

Frequent Releases Reduce Risk

Chris O'Dell

"Frequent releases reduce risk"—this is something you hear all the time in conversations about continuous delivery. How exactly is this the case? It sounds counterintuitive. Surely, releasing more often is introducing more volatility into production? Isn't it less risky to hold off releasing as long as possible, taking your time with testing to guarantee confidence in the package? Let's think about what we mean by *risk*.

What Is Risk?

Risk is a factor of the likelihood of a failure happening combined with the worst-case impact of that failure:

Risk = Likelihood of failure × Worst-case impact of failure

Therefore, an extremely low-risk activity is when failure is incredibly unlikely to happen and the impact of the failure is negligible. Low-risk activities also include those where either of these factors—likelihood or impact—is so low that it severely reduces the effect of the other.

Playing the lottery is low-risk: the chance of failing (i.e., not winning) is very high, but the impact of failing (i.e., losing the cost of the ticket) is minimal, so playing the lottery has few adverse consequences.

Flying is also low-risk due to the factors being balanced the opposite way. The chance of a failure is extremely low—flying has a very good safety record —but the impact of a failure is extremely high. We fly often, as we consider the risk to be very low.

High-risk activities are when both sides of the product are high—a high likelihood of failure and high impact. For example, they include extreme sports such as free solo climbing and cave diving.

Large, Infrequent Releases Are Riskier

Rolling a set of changes into a single release package increases the likelihood of a failure occurring—a lot of change is happening all at once.

The worst-case impact of a failure includes the release causing an outage, or severe data loss. Each change in a release could cause this to happen.

The reaction to try and test for every failure is a reasonable one, but it is impossible. We can test for the known scenarios, but we can't test for scenarios we don't know about until they are encountered (the "unknown unknowns").

This is not to say that testing is pointless—on the contrary, it provides confidence that the changes have not broken expected, known behavior. The tricky part is balancing the desire for thorough testing against the likelihood of tests finding a failure, and the time taken to perform and maintain them.

Build up an automated suite of tests that protect against the failure scenarios you know about. Each time a new failure is encountered, add it to the test suite. Increase your suite of regression tests, but keep them light, fast, and repeatable.

No matter how much you test, production is the only place where success counts. Small, frequent releases reduce the likelihood of a failure. A release containing as small a change as possible reduces the likelihood that the release will contain a failure.

There's no way to reduce the impact of a failure—the worst case is still that the release could bring the whole system down and incur severe data loss—but we lower the overall risk with the smaller releases.

Release small changes often to reduce the likelihood of a failure and, therefore, the risk of change.

From Puzzles to Products

Jessica Kerr

I went into programming because it was easy. I solved puzzles all day, then went home at five thirty and hung out with my friends. Twenty years later, I stay in software because it is hard.

It is hard because I moved from solving puzzles to growing products, from obsessing over correctness to optimizing for change.

Early in my career, I focused on one area of the system. My team leader gave me requirements for new features. This defined "correct," and when the code achieved it, my task was done.

The available means were restricted: we worked in C, with the standard library plus Oracle. For bonus points, we made the code look like everyone else's.

Within a few years, my perspective broadened: I met with customers; I participated in the negotiation between design and implementation. If a particular new feature took the code in an awkward direction, then we went back to the customer with other suggestions to solve the same problem. I now help define the puzzles, as well as solve them.

Puzzle solving is a prerequisite, not the essence of my work. The essence of my work is to provide a capability to the rest of the organization (or to the world); I do this by operating a useful product.

Puzzles have an end state as a goal—like a game of baseball, there is a fixed end. With products, the goal is to continue being useful—like a career in baseball, we want to keep playing.

Puzzles have defined means, like a board game. Growing products, we have the world of libraries and services, a plethora of puzzles solved for us. It is more like a game of pretend, open to what we can find.

Later in my career, my perspective broadened.

When I push satisfactory code, this is only the beginning of my work. I want more than code change: I aim for system change. A new feature in my app must work with the current systems that depend on mine. I work with the people who own those systems to help them start using the new feature.

Now I see my job as designing change, not code. Code is a detail.

Designing change means feature flags, backward compatibility, data migrations, and progressive deployment. It means documentation, helpful error messages, and social contact with adjacent teams.

A plus: all those `if` statements for feature flags, deprecated methods, and backward compatibility handling? These are no longer ugly. They express change—and change is the point, not some particular state of the code.

Designing change means building in observability so I can tell who is still using the deprecated feature, and who is getting value from the new one. In puzzle solving, I didn't have to care whether people liked the feature, or even whether it was in production. Growing a product, I care very much. From experience in production, we learn how to make our products more useful.

Products don't have one definition of "correct." Many things are definitely not correct, so we can be careful about "not broken." Beyond that, we aim for "better."

Growing a product is hard in different ways than solving puzzles. Instead of hard work followed by a feeling of accomplishment, there is a slog of mushy work, through ambiguity and politics and context. The reward is more than a feeling, though: it can have a real impact on your company and thereby the world. That is more satisfying than ordinary fun.

"Full-Stack Developer" Is a Mindset

Maciej Walkowiak

In 2007—the year I started working my first job as a Java developer—the spectrum of technologies involved in day-to-day web development was quite narrow. Relational databases were in most cases the only type of database a developer needed to know. Frontend development was limited to HTML and CSS, spiced with a bit of JavaScript. Java development itself meant primarily working with Hibernate plus either Spring or Struts. This set of technologies covered almost everything necessary for building applications at that time. Most Java developers were actually *full-stack* developers, though that term had not yet been coined.

Things have changed significantly since 2007. We started building more and more complex user interfaces and handling this complexity with advanced JavaScript frameworks. We now use NoSQL databases, and almost every one of them is very different from the others. We stream data with Kafka, message with RabbitMQ, and do a lot more. In many cases, we also are responsible for setting up or maintaining the infrastructure with Terraform or CloudFormation, and we use or even configure Kubernetes clusters. Overall complexity has grown to the point that we have separate positions for frontend developer, backend developer, and DevOps engineer. Is it still possible to be a full-stack developer? That depends on how you understand the term.

You can't be an expert in everything. Considering how much the Java ecosystem has grown, it's hard to even be an expert in Java itself. The good thing is that you don't *have* to be one. For many projects, especially in smaller companies, the most beneficial team setup is when each area of expertise is covered by at least one expert, but these experts don't limit themselves to working only on that one area. Developers specialized in developing backend services can write frontend code—even if the code isn't perfect—and the same thing goes for frontend developers. This helps move projects forward more quickly, as one person can develop a change that requires touching every layer of the application. It also leads to greater engagement during refinement meetings, as there are no tasks isolated only to a certain group of people.

Most importantly, not being strictly limited to one area changes how you approach tasks. There are no "It's not my job" discussions anymore—developers are encouraged to learn. Having one person go on vacation is not an issue because there are always others who can cover for them—maybe not as efficiently, and maybe with results that aren't quite as good, but enough to keep things moving forward. It also means that when there is a need to introduce a new technology to the stack, you don't need to find a new team member, because existing team members are already comfortable leaving the comfort zone of their expertise.

Full-stack developer is therefore a mindset. It's being senior and junior at the same time, with a *can-do* attitude.

Garbage Collection Is Your Friend

Holly Cummins

Poor old garbage collection. One of the unsung heroes of Java, often blamed, rarely praised. Before Java made garbage collection mainstream, programmers had little choice but to track all the memory they'd allocated manually, and deallocate it once nothing was using it anymore. This is hard. Even with discipline, manual deallocation is a frequent cause of memory leaks (if too late) and crashes (if too early).

Java GC (garbage collection) is often thought of as a necessary cost, and "reduce time spent in GC" is common performance guidance. However, modern garbage collection can be faster than `malloc/free`, and time spent in GC can speed everything up. Why? Garbage collectors do more than memory deallocation: they also handle the allocation of memory and the arrangement of objects in memory. A good memory management algorithm can make allocation efficient by reducing fragmentation and contention. It can also boost throughput and lower response times by rearranging objects.

Why does the location of an object in memory affect application performance? A high proportion of a program's execution time is spent stalled in hardware, waiting for memory access. Heap access is geologically slow compared to instruction processing, so modern computers use caches. When an object is fetched into a processor's cache, its neighbors are also brought in; if they happen to be accessed next, that access will be fast. Having objects that are used at the same time near each other in memory is called *object locality*, and it's a performance win.

The benefits of efficient allocation are more obvious. If the heap is fragmented, when a program tries to create an object, it will have a long search to find a chunk of free memory big enough, and allocation becomes expensive. As an experiment, you can force GC to compact more; it will massively increase GC overhead, but often application performance will improve.

GC strategies vary by JVM implementation, and each JVM offers a range of configurable options. JVM defaults are usually a good start, but it is worth understanding some of the mechanics and variations possible. Throughput may be traded off against latency, and workload affects the optimum choice.

Stop-the-world collectors halt all program activity so they can collect safely. Concurrent collectors offload collection work to application threads, so there are no global pauses; instead, each thread will experience tiny delays. Although they do not have obvious pauses, concurrent collectors are less efficient than stop-the-world ones, so they're suitable for applications where pauses would be noticed (such as music playback or a GUI).

Collection itself is done by copying or by marking and sweeping. With mark-and-sweep, the heap is crawled to identify free space, and new objects get allocated into those gaps. Copying collectors divide the heap into two areas. Objects are allocated in the "new space." When that space is full, its nongarbage contents are copied to the reserve space and the spaces are swapped. In a typical workload, most objects die young (this is known as the generational hypothesis). With short-lived objects, the copying step will be super fast (there's nothing to copy!). However, if objects hang around, collection will be inefficient. Copying collectors are great for immutable objects and a disaster with object pooling "optimizations" (usually a bad idea anyway). As a bonus, copying collectors compact the heap, which allows near-instant object allocation and fast object access (fewer cache misses).

When evaluating performance, it should be related to business value. Optimize transactions per second, mean service time, or worst-case latency. But don't try to micro-optimize time spent in GC, because time invested in GC can actually help program speed.

Get Better at Naming Things

Peter Hilton

> *What is above all needed is to let the meaning choose the word, and not the other way around...the worst thing one can do with words is surrender to them.*
>
> —George Orwell

Getting better at naming things improves the maintainability of the code you write more than anything else. There's more to maintainable code than good naming, but naming things is famously hard, and usually neglected. Fortunately, programmers like a challenge.

First, avoid names that are meaningless (`foo`) or too abstract (`data`), duplicated (`data2`) or vague (`DataManager`), abbreviated or short (`dat`). Single letters (`d`) are the worst of all. These names are ambiguous, which slows everyone down because programmers spend more time reading code than writing code.

Next, adopt guidelines for better names—words with precise meanings that make the code say what it means.

Use up to four words for each name, and don't use abbreviations (except for `id` and those you adopt from the problem domain). One word is rarely enough; using more than four is clumsy and stops adding meaning. Java programmers use long class names but often prefer short local variable names, even when they're worse.

Learn and use problem domain terminology—domain-driven design's *ubiquitous vocabulary*. This is often concise: in publishing, the correct term for text changes might be *revision* or *edit,* depending on who makes the change. Instead of making words up, read the topic's Wikipedia page, talk to people who work in that domain, and add the words they use to your glossary.

Replace plurals with collective nouns (e.g., rename `appointment_list` to `calendar`). More generally, enlarge your English vocabulary so you can make names shorter and more precise. This is harder if you're a non-native English speaker, but everyone has to learn the domain jargon anyway.

Rename pairs of entities with relationship names (for instance, rename company_person to employee, owner, shareholder). When this is a field, you're naming the relationship between the field's type and the class it's a member of. In general, it's often worth extracting a new variable, method, or class just so you can explicitly name it.

Java helps you with good naming because you name classes separately from objects. Don't forget to actually name your types instead of relying on primitive and JDK classes: instead of String, you should usually introduce a class with a more specific name, such as CustomerName. Otherwise, you need comments to document unacceptable strings, such as empty ones.

Don't mix up class and object names: rename a date field called dateCreated to created, and a Boolean field called isValid to valid, to avoid duplicate type noise. Give objects different names: instead of a Customer called customer, use a more specific name, such as recipient when sending a notification or reviewer when posting a product review.

The first step in naming is to apply the basic naming conventions, such as using noun phrases for class names. The next step is good naming technique using guidelines like these. But guidelines have limits. The JavaBeans specification taught a generation of Java programmers to break object encapsulation and use vague method names, like setRating when rate might be better, for example. You don't need to name methods that aren't imperative with verb phrases, as in builder APIs like Customer.instance().rating(FIVE_STARS).active(). In the end, naming mastery is about choosing which rules to break.

Hey Fred, Can You Pass Me the HashMap?

Kirk Pepperdine

Picture the scene: an old, cramped office with several old wooden desks set back-to-back. Each desk equipped with an old black rotary phone and ashtrays dotted about. On one of the desks is a black HashMap that contains an ArrayList filled with customer data. Sam, needing to contact Acme Inc., scans the office looking for the HashMap. Eyes darting, he spots the HashMap and shouts out, "Hey Fred, can you please pass me the HashMap?" Can you picture that…yup, I didn't think so…

An important part of writing a program is the development of a vocabulary. Each word in that vocabulary should be an expression of something that is part of the domain we're modeling. After all, it is this code expression of our model that others will have to read and understand. Consequently, our choice of vocabulary can either help or hinder understanding of our code. Oddly enough, the choice of vocabulary impacts much more than readability: the words we use affect how we think about the problem at hand, which, in turn, impacts the structure of our code, our choice of algorithms, how we shape our APIs, how well the system will fit our purpose, how easily it will be maintained and extended, and, finally, how well it will perform. Yes, the vocabulary we develop when writing code matters a lot. So much so that keeping a dictionary at hand can be strangely useful when writing code.

Returning to the ridiculous example, of course, no one would ask for the HashMap. You'd most likely draw a blank stare from Fred if you asked him to pass the HashMap. Yet when we look at how to model the domain, we hear about the need to look up customer contact data that is organized by name. That screams HashMap. If we dig deeper into the domain, then we'll likely discover that the contact information is written on an index card that is neatly packed away in a Rolodex. Replacing the word HashMap with the word Rolodex not only offers a better abstraction in our code but it will also have an immediate impact on how we think about the problem at hand, and it offers a better way to express our thoughts to the reader of our code.

The takeaway here is that technical classes rarely have a place in the vocabulary of the domains we're working in. Instead, what they offer are building blocks for deeper, more meaningful abstractions. The need for utility classes should be a red flag that you're missing an abstraction. Additionally, technical classes in APIs should also be a red flag.

For example, consider the case where a method signature takes a String to represent a first name and a String for a last name. These are used to look up data held in a HashMap:

```
return listOfNames.get(firstName + lastName);
```

The question is, what is the missing abstraction? Having two fields forming a key is commonly known as a *composite key*. Using this abstraction we get:

```
return listOfNames.get(new CompositeKey(firstName, lastName));
```

When you make this change in a benchmark, the code runs three times faster. I would argue it is also more expressive: using CompositeKey better expresses the essence of the problem at hand.

How to Avoid Null

Carlos Obregón

Tony Hoare calls null the "billion-dollar mistake." It's a mistake, and that's why you should get in the habit of forbidding code from using null. If you have a reference to an object that might be null, you have to remember to do a null check before trying to call any method of it. But since there's no obvious difference between a null reference and a non-null one, it's too easy to forget and get a NullPointerException.

The most future-proof way to avoid issues is to use an alternative when possible.

Avoid Initializing Variables to Null

It is usually not a good idea to declare a variable until you know what value it should hold. For complex initialization, move all the initialization logic to a method. For example, instead of doing this:

```
public String getEllipsifiedPageSummary(Path path) {
    String summary = null;
    Resource resource = this.resolver.resolve(path);
    if (resource.exists()) {
        ValueMap properties = resource.getProperties();
        summary = properties.get("summary");
    } else {
        summary = "";
    }
    return ellipsify(summary);
}
```

Do the following:

```
public String getEllipsifiedPageSummary(Path path) {
    var summary = getPageSummary(path);
    return ellipsify(summary);
}
```

```
public String getPageSummary(Path path) {
    var resource = this.resolver.resolve(path);
    if (!resource.exists()) {
        return "";
    }
    var properties = resource.getProperties();
    return properties.get("summary");
}
```

Initializing a variable to null might leak null unintentionally if you are not careful with your error-handling code. Another developer might change the control flow without realizing the issue—and that other developer might be you three months after the code was first written.

Avoid Returning Null

When you read the signature of a method, you should be able to understand if it always returns a T or if sometimes it doesn't. Returning an Optional<T> is a better option that makes the code more explicit. Optional's API makes it very easy to deal with the scenario where no T was produced.

Avoid Passing and Receiving Null Parameters

If you need a T, ask for it; if you can get by without one, then don't ask for it. For an operation that can have an optional parameter, create two methods: one with the parameter and one without.

For example, the method drawImage from the Graphics class in the JDK has a version that receives five parameters and a sixth parameter, an ImageObserver, which is optional. If you don't have an ImageObserver, you need to pass null like this:

```
g.drawImage(original, X_COORD, Y_COORD, IMG_WIDTH, IMG_HEIGHT, null);
```

It would have been better to have another method with just the first five parameters.

Acceptable Nulls

When is it acceptable to use null, then? As an implementation detail of a class, i.e., the value of an attribute. The code that needs to be aware of that absence of value is contained to the same file, and it's much more simple to reason about it and not leak null.

So remember, unless you have an attribute, it's always possible to avoid using null using a superior construct in your code. If you stop using null where you don't need it, then it becomes impossible to leak null and have a NullPointerException. And if you avoid these exceptions, you'll be part of the solution to the billion-dollar problem instead of being part of it.

How to Crash Your JVM

Thomas Ronzon

There are so many new APIs, cool libraries, and must-try techniques you need to know that it can be hard to stay up-to-date.

But is this really all you need to know as a Java developer? What about the environment your software is running in? Couldn't it be that a problem here could crash your software, and you wouldn't even be able to understand or find that problem because it's outside the world of libraries and code? Are you prepared to consider another perspective?

Here is a challenge: try to find ways to crash your Java Virtual Machine! (Or, at least, bring its normal execution to a sudden and unexpected stop.) The more ways you know, the better you understand your surroundings and appreciate what can go wrong with a running software system.

Here are a few to get you started:

1. Try to allocate as much memory as you can. RAM is not endless—if no more RAM can be allocated, your allocation will fail.

2. Try to write data to your hard disk until it is full. Same problem as with RAM: though bigger than RAM, disk space is not endless either.

3. Try to open as many files as you can. Do you know the maximum number of file descriptors for your environment?

4. Try to create as many threads as you can. On a Linux system, you can look at `/proc/sys/kernel/pid_max` and you will see how many processes may be running on your system. How many threads are you allowed to create on your system?

5. Try to modify your own *.class* files in the filesystem—the current run of your application will be its last!

6. Try to find your own process ID, and then try to kill it by using `Runtime.exec` (e.g., by calling `kill -9` on your process ID).

7. Try to create a class at runtime that only calls System.exit, load that class dynamically via the class loader, then call it.

8. Try to open as many socket connections as possible. On a Unix system, the maximum number of possible socket connections equals the maximum number of file descriptors (often 2,048). How many are available where your application is running?

9. Try to hack your system. Download an exploit via code or by using wget. Execute the exploit, and then call shutdown -h as root on a Unix system or shutdown /s as administrator on a Windows system.

10. Try jumping without a safety net. Part of Java's safety comes from its language design and part from the bytecode verification in your JVM. Run your JVM with -noverify or -Xverify:none, which disables all bytecode verification, and write something that would otherwise not be allowed to run.

11. Try using Unsafe. This backdoor class is used to get access to low-level facilities such as memory management. All the syntax of Java, all the safety of C!

12. Try going native. Write some native code. All the syntax of C, all the safety of C!

Try to find your own ways to crash your JVM and ask colleagues for their ideas. Also consider asking job interview candidates how they might go about this. Whatever their answer, you will soon learn whether the interviewee is able to see the world outside their IDE window.

P.S. If you find other creative ways to crash a JVM, please let me know!

Improving Repeatability and Auditability with Continuous Delivery

Billy Korando

Handcrafting is valued because of the time and effort involved and small imperfections that give character and uniqueness. While these qualities might be valued in food, furniture, or art, when it comes to delivering code, these qualities are serious impediments to an organization's success.

Humans are not well suited to performing repetitive tasks. No matter how detail-oriented a person might be, mistakes happen when performing the series of complex steps required to deploy an application. A step might be skipped, run in the wrong environment, or otherwise performed incorrectly, leading to a deployment failure.

When deployment failures happen, a considerable amount of time can be spent investigating what went wrong. This investigative process is hindered as manual processes often lack a central point of control and can be opaque. When a root cause is determined, the typical resolution is to add more layers of control to prevent the problem from happening again, but this usually only succeeds in making the deployment process more complicated and painful!

Organizations struggling to deliver code is not news, so to address this, organizations have begun to migrate to continuous delivery (CD). CD is an approach of automating the steps of delivering code to production. From the time when a developer commits a change to when that change is deployed to production, any step that can be automated, should be—testing, change control, the process of deployment, etc.

When migrating to CD, a primary motivation is to reduce the time and effort required to deploy code. While reduced time and effort are significant advantages to CD, they aren't the only ones! CD also improves the repeatability and auditability of your deployment process. Here is why you should care about these qualities.

Repeatable

Automating the steps to deploy code means scripting each step so it can be executed by a computer instead of a human. This greatly improves the repeatability of the deployment process, as computers excel at performing repetitive tasks.

A repeatable process is inherently less risky, which can encourage organizations to release more often and with smaller changesets. This can lead to second-order benefits of targeting a release to fix specific issues, such as performance. A release can contain only performance changes, which can make it possible to measure if those changes improved, degraded, or had no impact on performance.

Auditable

Automating deployments greatly improves transparency, which naturally improves auditability. The scripts used to execute steps and values supplied to them can be stored in version control, allowing for easy review. Automated deployments can also generate reports that can also help with auditing. The improved auditability of the deployment process is what moves CD from a niche concept for start-ups and non-mission-critical applications to essential in even the most tightly regulated and controlled industries.

When I first heard about CD, I found the deployments on demand concept intoxicating. After reading *Continuous Delivery* by Jez Humble and David Farley (Addison-Wesley), I learned that the reduced time and effort are in many ways secondary to the repeatability and auditability that CD offers. If your organization has been struggling to deliver code to production, I hope this can help build your case to management for why you should switch to CD.

In the Language Wars, Java Holds Its Own

Jennifer Reif

We all pick our favorites and downplay other options (colors, cars, sports teams, and so on). Programming language choice is not exempt. Whether it's the one we are most comfortable with or the one that got us a job, we cling to that choice.

Today, we will focus on Java. There are perfectly valid complaints and praises for this language. These are my experiences, and others may see things differently.

My History with Java

First, let's see the lens through which I view this language.

My introduction to programming applications was in college using—wait for it—Java. Prior to that, I had a couple of intro classes using HTML, Alice, and Visual Basic. None of those was designed to dive into complex code structures.

So, Java was my first exposure to programming for enterprise environments and critical processes. I've since had experience with many other languages, but I still go back to Java.

Java's Design and Background

Java was created in 1995 with a C-like syntax and following the WORA principle (write once, run anywhere). Its goal was to simplify complex programming required in C-family languages and achieve platform independence via the JVM.

I think knowing a language's history helps put positives and negatives into context, as understanding the background shows what the creators sacrificed to reach other goals.

Java's Downsides

Most complaints are that deployables are larger and the syntax is verbose. While valid, I think the previous paragraph on Java's history explains why these exist.

First, Java deployables are larger overall. As we saw in Java's history, it was created to "write once, run anywhere" so the same application could run on any JVM. This means all dependencies have to be included for deployment, whether rolled into a single JAR or across various components (WAR file + app server + JRE + dependencies). This affects the size of the deployment.

Second, Java is verbose. Again, I attribute this to its design. It was created when C and similar languages ruled the space, which required developers to specify low-level details. Java's goal was to be more user-friendly by abstracting some of those details.

Why I Like Java

- Java tells me what I am building and how. With other languages, I may be able to write something in fewer lines, but I'm less sure what it's doing under the hood, which I don't like as much.
- It's a widely applicable skill. Dealing with Java in various capacities has given me knowledge in both the business and the technical market. Java is not the only language with this benefit, but it seems the most enduring one with this property.
- Java allows me to play with technology in all stacks and areas. It seems to bridge all those. I like to dabble and explore, and Java has enabled that.

What Does It Mean for Developers?

The market is diverse, with many options fitting business needs. One size does not (and should not) fit all, so each developer needs to decide the best language for the job. Even if you don't favor Java as a primary language, I still think it's a valuable skill to have.

Inline Thinking

Patricia Aas

Computers changed. They changed in many ways, but for the purpose of this text they changed in one significant way: the relative cost of reading from RAM became extremely high.

This was something that happened gradually, until RAM accesses could completely dominate the performance metrics of an application. The CPU was constantly waiting for memory accesses to finish. And as the cost of going to RAM, relative to registers, grew and grew, chip manufacturers introduced more and more levels of cache and made them bigger and bigger.

And caches are great! If what you need is in them…

Caches are complex, but as a rule they will predict that a subsequent memory access will be close to, or preferably adjacent to, a recent, previous access. This is done by fetching a bit more than needed from memory and storing this excess in the cache, often called prefetching. If a later access can get its value from the cache instead of RAM, it is referred to as a "cache-friendly" access.

Imagine that you need to iterate through a big array of relatively small objects, maybe a bunch of triangles. In Java today, you don't really have an array of triangles; you have an array of pointers to triangle objects because regular objects in Java are "reference types," meaning you access them through Java pointers/references. So even though the array is probably a contiguous section of memory, the triangle objects themselves can be anywhere on the Java heap. Looping through this array will be "cache-unfriendly" since we will be jumping around in memory from triangle object to triangle object, and the cache prefetching will probably not help us much.

Imagine instead that the array contained the actual triangle objects, not pointers to them. Now they are close in memory, and looping over them is much more "cache-friendly." The next triangle might be waiting for us right there in the cache. Object types that can be stored directly into an array like that are called "value types" or "inline types." Java already has several inline types, for example `int` and `char`, and will soon have user-defined ones, probably called "inline classes." These will be similar to regular classes but simpler.

Another way to be cache-friendly is to store objects in your stack frame or directly in registers. A difference between inline types and reference types is that you don't have to allocate inline types on the heap. This is useful for objects that live only for the scope of this method call. Since the relevant parts of the stack are probably in the cache, access to objects on the stack will tend to be cache-friendly. As a bonus, objects that are not allocated on the Java heap do not need to be garbage collected.

These cache-friendly behaviors are already present in Java when using so-called "primitive types," like `int`s and `char`s. Primitive types are inline types and come with all of their advantages. So even though inline types may seem foreign in the beginning, you have worked with them before; you just might not have thought of them as objects. So, when "inline classes" seem confusing, you could try thinking, "What would an `int` do?"

Interop with Kotlin

Sebastiano Poggi

In recent years, Kotlin has been a hot-button topic in the JVM community; the usage of the language is constantly increasing, from mobile to backend projects. One of Kotlin's advantages is its great degree of interoperability with Java right off the bat.

Calling into any Java code from Kotlin just works. Kotlin understands Java perfectly well, but there's one minor annoyance that may present itself if you're not following Java best practices to the letter: the lack of non-nullable types in Java. If you don't apply nullability annotations in Java, Kotlin assumes all those types have unknown nullability—they're so-called platform types. If you're certain they will never be null, you can coerce them into a non-null type with the !! operator or by casting them to a non-null type. In either case, you'll get a crash if the value is null at runtime. The best way to handle this scenario is to add nullability annotations such as @Nullable and @NotNull to your Java APIs. There are a variety of supported annotations (*https://oreil.ly/hKoXx*): JetBrains, Android, JSR-305, FindBugs, and more. This way, Kotlin will know the type nullability, and when coding in Java you'll receive additional IDE insights and warnings about potential nulls. Win-win!

When invoking Kotlin code from Java, you should find that while the majority of the code will work just fine, you may see quirks with some advanced Kotlin language features that don't have a direct equivalent in Java. The Kotlin compiler has to adopt some creative solutions to implement them in bytecode. These are hidden when in Kotlin, but Java isn't aware of these mechanisms and lays them bare, resulting in a usable but suboptimal API.

Top-level declarations are an example. Since the JVM bytecode doesn't support methods and fields outside of classes, the Kotlin compiler puts them in a synthetic class with the same name as the file they're in. For example, all top-level symbols in a *FluxCapacitor.kt* file will appear as static members of the FluxCapacitorKt class, from Java. You can change the synthetic class name to something nicer by annotating the Kotlin file with `@file:JvmName("Flux CapacitorFuncs")`.

You may expect members defined in a (`companion`) object to be static in bytecode, but that's not the case. Kotlin under the hood moves them into a field named `INSTANCE`, or a synthetic `Companion` inner class. If you need to access them as static members, just annotate them with `@JvmStatic`. You can also make (`companion`) object properties appear as fields in Java by annotating them as `@JvmField`.

Lastly, Kotlin offers optional parameters with default values. It's a very convenient feature, but unfortunately, Java doesn't support it. In Java, you need to provide values for all the parameters, including the ones that are supposed to be optional. To avoid this, you can use the `@JvmOverloads` annotation, which tells the compiler to generate telescopic overloads for all optional parameters. Ordering of the parameters is important as you don't get all possible permutations in the overloads, but rather one extra overload for each optional parameter, in the order in which they appear in Kotlin.

To summarize, Kotlin and Java are almost entirely interoperable out of the box: that's one of Kotlin's advantages over other JVM languages. In some scenarios, though, a minute of work on your APIs will make its usage much more pleasant from the other language. There's really no reason not to go the extra mile, given how big of an impact you can make with such little effort!

It's Done, But...

Jeanne Boyarsky

How many times have you been to a stand-up, daily Scrum or status meeting and heard the phrase "It's done, but..."? When I hear that, my first thought is "So, it's not done." There are three issues with using the word *done* when it isn't done.

1. Communication and Clarity

Ideally your team has a *definition of done*. But even if they don't, there is probably some expectation of what *done* means. And, even better, the person reporting on status knows that. Otherwise, we wouldn't have a disclaimer on the task's done-ness.

Common things that aren't *done* include writing tests, documentation, and edge cases. Take a moment and see if you can think of any more. Similarly, I don't like the term *done done*. It implicitly blesses the idea that done doesn't actually mean *done*. Be a clear communicator. If something isn't done, don't say it's done.

This is an opportunity for you to convey more information. For example, "I coded the happy path and next I will add validation" or "I finished all the code—the only thing remaining is for me to update the user manual" or even "I thought I was done and then discovered the widget doesn't work on Tuesdays." All of these give information to your team.

2. Perception

Managers like hearing the word *done*. It means you are free to take on more work. Or help a teammate. Or pretty much anything that does not include spending more time on the task. As soon as they hear *done*, that becomes the perception. The *but* either gets forgotten or becomes a small thing.

Now you are moving on to the next thing when you didn't finish the first thing. That's where technical debt comes from! Sometimes technical debt is a choice. However, making that choice by discussing it is far better than having it made for you because you claimed to be done.

OK. I'm done with this article, but I still have to write the last part. See how that worked? I'm not actually done at all.

3. There's No Partial Credit for Done

Done is a binary state. It's either done or it isn't. There's no such thing as half done. Suppose you are building a pair of stilts and say you are 50% done. Think about what that means. It could mean you have one stilt. Not particularly useful. More likely it means that you think you have one stilt but still have to build the other one and then test. Testing is likely to reveal that you have to go back and change something. This rework means you weren't even 50% done. You were optimistic.

Remember: don't say you are done until you are *done*!

Java Certifications: Touchstone in Technology

Mala Gupta

Imagine you need to undergo a robotic surgery. The surgeon is experienced and qualified but has no credentials with robotic equipment for surgery. Would you still move forward with the robotic surgery with that surgeon? Unless I was convinced of the surgeon's skills on robotic equipment, I wouldn't.

Taking the analogy further, how would you ascertain a candidate's skills before adding them to your critical projects? A university degree in computer science is not enough. The gap in skills gained through a university curriculum and a job's requirements is wide.

Independent skill training organizations are stepping in to bridge this gap. But it is not enough. Who would measure the quality of their content and how? This is where the industry steps in.

An apt metaphor would be the touchstone—the wonderstone used in ancient times to measure the purity of gold and other precious metals that were used as currency. A metal coin was rubbed against a dark siliceous stone like jasper, and a colorful residue would be indicative of the metal's purity.

Organizations like Oracle have defined these benchmarks in the form of professional certifications, to play the role of touchstones, measuring IT skills in a standardized manner.

People often ask whether these professional certifications are necessary for computer science graduates or postgraduates. Has the university curriculum covered the content already? Here one needs to put the short-term and long-term objectives in perspective. Graduation or postgraduation in computer science at a university can be a strategic choice to chalk out a long-term career path, whereas earning professional certifications are tactical choices to gain proven skills in technologies that need to be applied in immediate projects and achieve short-term goals.

Professional certifications in Java by the Oracle Corporation are in great demand. They are awarded when a candidate meets the defined requirements. Depending on the certification, a candidate may be required to complete a course or project, or pass an examination. The purpose is to establish that the individual is qualified to hold certain types of positions or work on certain projects. Certified skills bridge the gap between their existing skills and skills required by the industry, resulting in a higher rate of success on projects. These certifications are regularly updated.

Oracle offers multiple options in Java certifications, which define topics and a pathway to be followed by developers. Developers can choose the right certification as per their interest.

Validated skills establish the credibility of an individual's ability in programming in a particular language or their understanding of a platform, methodology, or practice to prospective employers. They help professionals to clear the initial hurdle of résumé reviews and selections for interviews.

Java certifications help an individual advance in their career. When people are searching for jobs and organizations and teams are trying to find talent with verified skills, these certifications can be a first step.

Java Is a '90s Kid

Ben Evans

There are only two kinds of languages: the ones people complain about and the ones nobody uses.

　　—Bjarne Stroustrup

Whether Stroustrup's insight says more about programming languages or human nature, I'm not sure. However, it does draw attention to the often-forgotten truism that the design of programming languages is a human endeavor. As such, languages always carry traces of the environment and context in which they were created.

So it shouldn't come as a surprise that traces of the late 1990s can be seen everywhere in the design of Java, if you know where to look.

For example, the sequence of bytes to load an object reference from local variable 0 onto the temporary evaluation stack is this two-byte sequence:

```
19 00 // aload 00
```

However, the JVM's bytecode instruction set provides a variant form that is one byte shorter:

```
2A // aload_0
```

One byte saved may not sound like much, but it can start to add up over an entire class file.

Now, remember, in the late '90s, Java classes (often applets) were downloaded over dial-up modems, incredible devices that were capable of reaching blistering speeds of 14.4 kilobits per second. With that kind of bandwidth, saving bytes wherever possible was a huge motivation for Java.

You could even argue that the entire concept of *primitive types* is a combination of a performance hack and a sop to C++ programmers newly arrived in the Java world—products of the 1990s, when Java was created.

Even the "magic number" (the first few bytes of a file, which allow the operating system to identify the file type) for all Java class files feels dated:

```
CA FE BA BE
```

"Cafe babe" is maybe not a great look for Java today. Unfortunately, it's not something that can realistically be changed now.

It's not only the bytecode: in the Java standard library (especially the older parts of it), APIs that replicate equivalent C APIs are everywhere. Every programmer who's been forced to read the contents of a file by hand knows that only too well. Worse yet, the mere mention of `java.util.Date` is enough to break many Java programmers out in a rash.

Through the lens of 2020 and beyond, Java is sometimes seen as a mainstream, middle-of-the-road language. What that narrative misses is that the world of software has radically changed since Java's debut. Big ideas such as virtual machines, dynamic self-management, JIT compilation, and garbage collection are now part of the general landscape of programming languages.

Though some may view Java as The Establishment, it's really the mainstream that has moved to encompass the space where Java has always been. Underneath the veneer of enterprise respectability, Java is still a '90s kid.

Java Programming from a JVM Performance Perspective

Monica Beckwith

Tip #1: Don't Obsess Over Garbage

I find that sometimes Java developers obsess over the amount of garbage their applications produce. Very few cases warrant this sort of obsession. A garbage collector (GC) helps the Java Virtual Machine (JVM) in memory management. For OpenJDK HotSpot VM, the GC along with the dynamic just-in-time (JIT) tiered compiler (client (C1) + server class (C2)) and the interpreter make up its execution engine. There are a slew of optimizations that a dynamic compiler can perform on your behalf. For example, C2 can utilize dynamic branch prediction and have a probability ("always" or "never") for code branches taken (or not). Similarly, C2 excels in optimizations related to constants, loops, copies, deoptimizations, and so on.

Trust the adaptive compiler, but when in doubt verify using "serviceability," "observability," logging, and all the other such tools that we have thanks to our rich ecosystem.

What matters to a GC is an object's liveness/age, its "popularity," the "live set size" for your application, the long-lived transients, allocation rate, marking overhead, your promotion rate (for the generational collector), and so forth.

Tip #2: Characterize and Validate Your Benchmarks

A peer of mine once brought in some observations of a benchmarking suite with various sub-benchmarks. One of these was characterized as a "start-up and related" benchmark. After taking a look at the performance numbers and the premise that was the comparison between OpenJDK 8u and OpenJDK 11u LTS releases, I realized that the difference in numbers could have been due to the default GC changing from Parallel GC to G1 GC. So, it seems that the (sub-)benchmark either was not properly characterized or wasn't validated. Both are important benchmarking exercises and help identify and isolate the "unit of test" (UoT) from other components of the test system that could act as detractors.

Tip #3: Allocation Size and Rate Still Matter

In order to be able to get to the bottom of the issue discussed above, I asked to see the GC logs. Within minutes, it was clear that the (fixed) region size, which is based on the heap size of the application, was categorizing the "regular" objects as "humongous." For the G1 GC, humongous objects are objects that span 50% or more of a G1 region. Such objects don't follow the fast path for allocations and are allocated out of the old generation. Hence, allocation size matters for regionalized GCs.

A GC keeps up with the live object graph mutation and moves objects from the "From" space into the "To" space. If your application is allocating at a rate faster than your GC's (concurrent) marking algorithm can keep up with, then that can become a problem. Also, a generational GC may prematurely promote short-lived objects or not age transients properly due to the influx of allocations. OpenJDK's G1 GC is still working on not being dependent on its fallback, fail-safe, nonincremental, full heap traversing, (parallel) stop-the-world collector.

Tip #4: An Adaptive JVM Is Your Right and You Should Demand It

It's great to see an adaptive JIT and all the advancements geared toward start-up, ramp-up, JIT availability, and footprint optimizations. Similarly, various GC-level algorithmic smartness is available. Those GCs that aren't there yet should get there soon, but that won't happen without our help. As Java developers, please provide feedback on your use case to the community and help drive innovation in this area. Also, do test out the features that are continually getting added to the JIT.

Java Should Feel Fun

Holly Cummins

I started my Java career using J2EE 1.2. I had questions. Why were there four classes and hundreds of lines of generated code for each bean? Why did compiling tiny projects take half an hour? It wasn't productive, and it wasn't fun. Those two often go together: things feel un-fun because we know they're *waste*. Think about meetings where nothing is decided, status reports no one reads...

If un-fun is bad, what *is* fun? Is it good? And how do we get it? Fun can have different faces:

- Exploration (focused investigation)
- Play (for its own sake, no goal)
- Puzzles (rules and a goal)
- Games (rules and a winner)
- Work (a satisfying goal)

Java allows all of these—the work part is obvious, and anyone who's debugged a Java program knows about the puzzle part. (Debugging isn't necessarily fun, but finding the solution is *great*.) We learn through exploration (when we're new to something) and play (when we know enough to do stuff).

Leaving aside the fun we can have with it, is Java inherently fun? Java *is* verbose compared to younger languages. Boilerplate isn't fun, but some of it is fixable. For example, Lombok neatly generates getters and setters, as well as `hashCode` and `equals` methods (tedious and error-prone otherwise). Manually writing entry and exit trace is un-fun, but aspects or tracing libraries can instrument dynamically (and massively improve code readability).

What makes something fun to use? In part it's about being expressive and understandable, but there's more to it than that. I'm not convinced lambdas are generally shorter or clearer than class-based alternatives. But they're fun!

When Java 8 came out, developers dove into lambdas like kids in a ball pit. We wanted to learn how it worked (exploration) and the challenge of expressing algorithms in a functional style (puzzles).

With Java, the fun thing to do is often also the best thing (win). Autoinstrumenting trace bypasses un-fun, eliminating method-name copy-and-paste errors and improving clarity. Or consider performance. For niche scenarios, weird, complicated code is needed to scrape every inch of speed. In most cases, however, the simplest code is also the *fastest*. (Which is not necessarily true for languages like C.) The Java JIT optimizes code as it runs; it's smartest for clean, idiomatic code. Straightforward code is nicely readable, so errors will be more obvious.

Misery-making code has a knock-on effect. Psychological research shows happiness and workplace success go together. One study (*https://oreil.ly/ pmfaZ*) showed that people with a positive mindset were 31% more productive than those with neutral or negative mindsets. You'll achieve less using poorly designed libraries, and then you'll continue to achieve less afterward because the bad code made you miserable.

Is "fun is good" an excuse to be irresponsible? Not at all! Consider whether everyone is having fun: *everyone* includes customers, colleagues, and future maintainers of your code. Compared to dynamically typed scripting languages, which can be fast and loose, Java already ticks the safe and responsible box. But the programs we write also need to be responsibly coded.

The good news is that for almost all boring tasks, computers can do the job faster and more correctly than people. Computers don't expect to have fun (yet), so take advantage of them! Don't accept tedium. If something seems un-fun, look for a better way. If there isn't one, invent one. We're programmers: we can fix boring.

Java's Unspeakable Types

Ben Evans

What is null?

New Java programmers often struggle with this idea. A simple example reveals the truth:

```
String s = null;
Integer i = null;
Object o = null;
```

The symbol null must therefore be a value.

As every value in Java has a type, null must therefore have a type. What is it?

It obviously cannot be any type that we ordinarily encounter. A variable of type String cannot hold a value of type Object—the Liskov substitution properties simply do not work that way.

Nor does Java 11 local variable type inference help:

```
jshell> var v = null;
| Error:
| cannot infer type for local variable v
| (variable initializer is 'null')
| var v = null;
| ^ - - - - - -^
```

The pragmatic Java programmer may simply scratch their head and decide, as many have done, that it doesn't really matter all that much. Instead, they can pretend "null is merely a special literal that can be of any reference type."

However, for those of us who find this approach unsatisfying, the true answer can be found in the Java Language Specification (JLS), in Section 4.1:

> There is also a special null type, the type of the expression null (§3.10.7, §15.8.1), which has no name.

Because the null type has no name, it is impossible to declare a variable of the null type or to cast to the null type.

There it is. Java allows us to write down values whose types we cannot declare as the types of variables. We might call these "unspeakable types" or, formally, *nondenotable types*.

As null shows, we've actually been using them all along. There are two more obvious places where this sort of types appear. The first arrived in Java 7, and the JLS has this to say about them:

An exception parameter may denote its type as either a single class type or a union of two or more class types (called alternatives).

The true type of a multicatch parameter is the union of the distinct possible types being caught. In practice, only code that conforms to the API contract of the *nearest common supertype* of the alternatives will compile. The real type of the parameter is not something we can use as the type of a variable.

In the following, what is the type of o?

```
jshell> var o = new Object() {
...> public void bar() { System.out.println("bar!"); }
...> }
o ==> $0@3bfdc050jshell> o.bar();
bar!
```

It can't be Object, because we can call bar() on it, and the Object type has no such method. Instead, the true type is nondenotable—it doesn't have a name we can use as the type of a variable in Java code. At runtime, the type is just a compiler-assigned placeholder ($0 in our example).

By using var as a "magic type," the programmer can preserve type information for each distinct usage of var, until the end of the method. We cannot carry the types from method to method. To do so, we would have to declare the return type—and that's precisely what we can't do!

The applicability of these types is therefore restricted—Java's type system remains very much a nominal system, and it seems unlikely that true structural types will ever appear in the language.

Finally, we should point out that many of the more advanced uses of generics (including the mysterious "capture of ?" errors) are really best understood in terms of nondenotable types as well—but that's another story.

The JVM Is a Multiparadigm Platform: Use This to Improve Your Programming

Russel Winder

Java is an imperative language: Java programs tell the JVM what to do and when to do it. But computing is all about building abstractions. Java is touted as an object-oriented language: the abstractions of Java are objects, methods, and message passing via method call. Over the years, people have built larger and larger systems using objects, methods, updatable state, and explicit iteration, and the cracks have appeared. Many are "papered over" using high quality testing, but still programmers end up "hacking" to get around various problems.

With the arrival of Java 8, Java underwent an extremely revolutionary change: it introduced method references, lambda expressions, default methods on interfaces, higher order functions, implicit iteration, and various other things. Java 8 introduced a very different way of thinking about the implementation of algorithms.

Imperative and declarative thinking are very different ways of expressing algorithms. During the 1980s and 1990s, these mindsets were seen as being distinct and irreconcilable: we had the object-oriented versus functional programming war. Smalltalk and C++ were the champions of object-orientation, and Haskell was the champion of functional. Later, C++ stopped being an object-oriented language and marketed itself as a multiparadigm language; Java took over as the champion of object-oriented. With Java 8, though, Java has become multiparadigm.

Back in the early 1990s, the JVM was constructed as the way of making Java portable—we can gloss over the history of the Green project and the Oak programming language. Initially, this was for making web browser plug-ins, but it rapidly moved to creating server-side systems. Java compiles to hardware-independent JVM bytecode, and an interpreter executes the bytecode. Just-in-time (JIT) compilers enable the whole interpretation model to execute much faster without changing the computational model of the JVM.

As the JVM became the hugely popular platform it is, other languages were created that made use of the bytecode as a target platform: Groovy, JRuby, and Clojure are dynamic languages using the JVM for execution; Scala, Ceylon, and Kotlin are static languages. Scala, in particular, showed in the late 2000s that object-orientation and functional programming can be integrated into a single, multiparadigm language. While Clojure is a functional language, Groovy and JRuby were multiparadigm from the outset. Kotlin is taking the lessons of Java, Scala, Groovy, etc. to create languages for the 2010s and 2020s on the JVM.

To use the JVM to its best effect, we should choose the right programming language for the problem. This doesn't necessarily mean one language for the whole problem: we can use different languages for different bits—all because of the JVM. So, we can use Java or Kotlin for the bits that are best expressed as static code, and Clojure or Groovy for the bits that are best handled by dynamic code. Trying to write dynamic code in Java is a pain, so use the right tool for the job given that all the programming languages can interoperate on the JVM.

Keep Your Finger on the Pulse

Trisha Gee

I learned Java version 1.1 at university (I wish this was because my university was using old technology instead of it being because I'm old). At that time Java was small enough, and I was naïve enough, that it was possible to believe I had learned all the Java I needed to know, and that I was set for life as a Java programmer.

During my first job, while I was still at university and had been using Java for less than a year, Java 1.2 was released. It had an entirely different user interface (UI) library, called Swing (*https://oreil.ly/6bJM0*), so I spent that summer learning Swing in order to use it to provide our users with a better experience.

A couple of years later, in my first job as a graduate, I discovered that applets were out and servlets were in. I spent the next six months learning about servlets and JSPs (*https://oreil.ly/G_LNk*) so we could give our users an online registration form.

In my next job, I found out that apparently we didn't use Vector (*https://oreil.ly/uFBk4*) any more—we used ArrayList (*https://oreil.ly/VrWT3*). This shook me to my core. How can the very fundamentals of the language, the data structures themselves, be changing underneath me? My first two discoveries involved learning additions to the language. This third one was about changes to things I thought I already knew. If I wasn't at university anymore being taught things, how was I supposed to just know this stuff?

I was fortunate in those early jobs to have people around me who were aware of the technology changes that impacted the Java projects I worked on. That should be the role of senior team members—not simply to do what they're told but to make suggestions on how to do it and to help the rest of the team improve too.

To survive as a Java programmer, you need to accept that Java is not a stationary language. It evolves, not only into new versions but as libraries, frameworks, and even new JVM languages. At first, this can be intimidating and overwhelming. But staying up-to-date doesn't mean you have to learn everything that's out there—it just means keeping your finger on the pulse, listening for common keywords, and understanding technology trends. You only need to drill down deeper when it's relevant for your job or when it's something that's personally interesting to you (or ideally both).

Knowing what's available in the current version of Java and what is planned for upcoming ones can help you implement features or functionality that will help your users do what they need to do. Which means it helps you as a developer be more productive. Java now releases a new version every six months. Keeping your finger on that pulse can actually make your life easier.

Kinds of Comments

Nicolai Parlog

Assume you want to put some comments into your Java code. Do you use /**, /*, or //? And where exactly do you put them? Beyond syntax, there are established practices that attach semantics to which is used where.

Javadoc Comments for Contracts

Javadoc comments (the ones enclosed in /** ... */) are exclusively used on classes, interfaces, fields, and methods and are placed directly above them. Here is an example from `Map::size`:

```
/**
 * Returns the number of key-value mappings in this map. If the
 * map contains more than Integer.MAX_VALUE elements, returns
 * Integer.MAX_VALUE.
 *
 * @return the number of key-value mappings in this map
 */
int size();
```

The example demonstrates syntax as well as semantics: *a Javadoc comment is a contract*. It promises API users what they can expect while keeping the type's central abstraction intact by not talking about implementation details. At the same time, it binds implementers to provide the specified behavior.

Java 8 relaxed this strictness a little while formalizing different interpretations by introducing the (nonstandardized) tags @apiNote, @implSpec, and @implNote. The prefixes, api or impl, specify whether the comment addresses users or implementers. The suffixes, Spec or Note, clarify whether this is actually a specification or only for illustration. Notice how @apiSpec is missing? That's because the comment's untagged text is supposed to fulfill that role: specifying the API.

Block Comments for Context

Block comments are enclosed in /* ... */. There are no restrictions on where to put them, and tools usually ignore them. A common way to use them is at the beginning of a class or even a method to give insights into its implementation. These can be technical details but can also outline the context in which the code was created (the famous *why* from *code tells you what, comments tell you why*) or paths not taken. A good example for providing implementation details can be found in HashMap, which starts like this:

```
/*
 * Implementation notes.
 *
 * This map usually acts as a binned (bucketed) hash table,
 * but when bins get too large, they are transformed into bins
 * of TreeNodes, each structured similarly to those in
 * java.util.TreeMap.
 * [...]
 */
```

As a rule of thumb, when your first solution isn't your last, when you make a trade-off, or when a weird requirement or a dependency's awkward API shapes your code, consider documenting that context. Your colleagues and your future self will thank you. (Silently.)

Line Comments for Weird Things

Line comments start with a //, which must be repeated on every line. There are no restrictions on where to use them, but it is common to put them above the commented line or block (as opposed to at the end). Tools ignore them—many developers do as well. Line comments are often used to narrate what the code does, which has rightfully been identified as a bad practice in general. It can still be helpful in specific cases, such as where the code has to use arcane language features or is easy to break in a subtle way (concurrency is the prime example for this).

Last Words

- Make sure to pick the right kind of comment.
- Don't break expectations.
- Comment your &#!*@$ code!

Know Thy flatMap

Daniel Hinojosa

Job titles morph constantly. As in the medical community, where the focus may be broader or more specialized, some of us who were once *just* programmers are now filling other job titles. One of the newest specialized disciplines is *data engineer*. The data engineer shepherds in the data, building pipelines, filtering data, transforming it, and molding it into what they or others need to make real-time business decisions with stream processing.

Both the general programmer and data engineer must master the `flatMap`, one of the most important tools for any functional, capable language like our beloved Java, but also for big data frameworks and streaming libraries. `flatMap`, like its partners `map` and `filter`, is applicable for anything that is a "container of something"—for example, `Stream<T>` and `CompletableFuture<T>`. If you want to look beyond the standard library, there is also `Observable<T>` (RXJava) and `Flux<T>` (Project Reactor).

In Java, we will use `Stream<T>`. The idea for `map` is simple—take all elements of a stream or collection and apply a function to it:

```
Stream.of(1, 2, 3, 4).map(x -> x * 2).collect(Collectors.toList())
```

This produces:

```
[2, 4, 6, 8]
```

What happens if we do the following?

```
Stream.of(1, 2, 3, 4)
    .map(x -> Stream.of(-x, x, x + 1))
    .collect(Collectors.toList())
```

Unfortunately, we get a `List` of `Stream` pipelines:

```
[java.util.stream.ReferencePipeline$Head@3532ec19,
 java.util.stream.ReferencePipeline$Head@68c4039c,
 java.util.stream.ReferencePipeline$Head@ae45eb6,
 java.util.stream.ReferencePipeline$Head@59f99ea]
```

But, thinking about it, of course for every element of the Stream we're creating another Stream. And take a deeper look in the map(x -> Stream.of(...)). For every singular element, we're creating a plural. If you perform a map with a plural, it's time to break out the flatMap:

```
Stream.of(1, 2, 3, 4)
    .flatMap(x -> Stream.of(-x, x, x+1))
    .collect(Collectors.toList())
```

That will produce what we were aiming for:

```
[-1, 1, 2, -2, 2, 3, -3, 3, 4, -4, 4, 5]
```

The opportunities for using flatMap are immense.

Let's move on to something more challenging that is apt for any functional programming or data engineering task. Consider the following relationship, where getters, setters, and toString are elided:

```
class Employee {
    private String firstName, lastName;
    private Integer yearlySalary;
    // getters, setters, toString
}
class Manager extends Employee {
    private List<Employee> employeeList;
    // getters, setters, toString
}
```

Suppose we are given only a Stream<Manager> and our goal is to determine all the salaries of all employees, including Managers and their Employees. We might be tempted to jump right to the forEach and start digging through those salaries. This, unfortunately, would model our code to the structure of the data and would cause needless complexity. A better solution would be to go the opposite way and structure the data to that of our code. That is where flatMap comes in:

```
List.of(manager1, manager2).stream()
    .flatMap(m ->
      Stream.concat(m.getEmployeeList().stream(), Stream.of(m)))
    .distinct()
    .mapToInt(Employee::getYearlySalary)
    .sum();
```

This code takes every manager and returns a plural—the manager and their employees. We then `flatMap` these collections to make one `Stream` and perform a `distinct` to filter out all duplicates. Now we can treat them all as one collection. The rest is easy. First we perform a Java-specific call, `map ToInt`, that extracts their `yearlySalary` and returns an `IntStream`, a specialized `Stream` type for integers. Finally, we sum the `Stream`. Concise code.

Whether you use `Stream` or another kind of `C<T>`, where `C` is any stream or collection, keep processing your data using `map`, `filter`, `flatMap`, or `groupBy` before reaching for the `forEach` or any other terminal operation like `collect`. If you go with the terminal operation prematurely, you'll lose any laziness and optimization that Java `Streams`, streaming libraries, or big data frameworks grant you.

Know Your Collections

Nikhil Nanivadekar

Collections are a staple in any programming language. They constitute one of the basic building blocks of commonly developed code. The Java language introduced the Collections framework a long time ago in JDK 1.2. Many programmers reach for `ArrayList` as their de facto collection to use. However, there's more to collections than `ArrayList`, so let's explore.

Collections can be classified as *ordered* or *unordered*. Ordered collections have a predictable iteration order; unordered collections do not have a predictable iteration order. Another way to classify collections is *sorted* or *unsorted*. The elements in a sorted collection are sequenced from start to end based on a comparator; unsorted collections have no particular sequence based on elements. Although *sorted* and *ordered* have similar meanings in English, they cannot always be used interchangeably for collections. The important distinction is that ordered collections have a predictable iteration order but no sort order. Sorted collections have a predictable sort order, hence they have a predictable iteration order. Remember: all sorted collections are ordered collections, but not all ordered collections are sorted collections. There are various ordered, unordered, sorted, and unsorted collections in the JDK. Let's take a look at a few of them.

`List` is an interface for ordered collections with a stable indexing order. Lists allow duplicate elements to be inserted and provide a predictable iteration order. The JDK offers `List` implementations like `ArrayList` and `Linked List`. To find a particular element, the `contains` method can be used. The `contains` operation traverses the list from the beginning, hence finding elements in a `List` is an O(*n*) operation.

`Map` is an interface that maintains key-to-value relationships, and retains only unique keys. If the same key and different value is added to a map, the old value is replaced by the new value. The JDK offers `Map` implementations like `HashMap`, `LinkedHashMap`, and `TreeMap`. A `HashMap` is unordered, whereas a `LinkedHashMap` is ordered; both rely on `hashCode` and `equals` to determine unique keys. A TreeMap is sorted: the keys are sorted according to a compara tor or by the sort order of Comparable keys. TreeMap relies on compareTo to determine sort order and uniqueness of keys. To find a particular element, Map provides the containsKey and containsValue methods. For HashMap, containsKey looks up the key in the internal hash table. If the look-up results in a non-null object, it is checked for equality with the object passed to containsKey. The containsValue operation traverses all the values from the beginning. Hence, finding keys in a HashMap is an O(1) operation, whereas finding values in a HashMap is an O(n) operation.

Set is an interface for collections of unique elements. In the JDK, sets are backed by maps where the keys are the elements and values are null. The JDK offers Set implementations like HashSet (backed by HashMap), Linked HashSet (backed by LinkedHashMap), and TreeSet (backed by TreeMap). To find a particular element, the contains method can be used for Set. The con tains method on a Set delegates to containsKey of a Map and therefore is an O(1) operation.

Collections are an important piece of a software puzzle. To use them effectively, it is necessary to understand their functionality, their implementation, and last but not least, the implications of using an iteration pattern. Remember to read the documentation, and write tests while using these versatile and basic building blocks of code.

Kotlin Is a Thing

Mike Dunn

Java is maybe the most mature and vetted language still in common use, and that is unlikely to change dramatically in the foreseeable future. To facilitate modern notions of what a programming language should do, some smart folks decided to write a new language that did all the Java Things, plus some cool new Things that would be fairly painless to learn and be largely interoperable. Someone like me, who's been working on the same huge Android app for years, can decide to write a single class in Kotlin without committing to a complete migration.

Kotlin is meant to let you write shorter, cleaner, more modern code. While modern and preview versions of Java do address a lot of the issues Kotlin manages, Kotlin can be especially useful for Android developers, who are stuck somewhere between Java 7 and Java 8.

Let's look at a few examples, like Kotlin's property constructor pattern for models, starting with a simple example of what a Java model may look like:

```
public class Person {
  private String name;
  private Integer age;
  public String getName() {
    return name;
  }
  public void setName(String name) {
    this.name = name;
  }
  public Integer getAge() {
    return age;
  }
  public void setAge(int age) {
    this.age = age;
  }
}
```

We could create a special constructor to take some initial values:

```java
public class Person {
  public Person(String name, Integer age) {
    this.name = name;
    this.age = age;
  }
  ...
}
```

Not too bad, but you can probably see how a few more properties could make the definition for this pretty simple class get bloated really quickly. Let's take a look at that class in Kotlin:

```kotlin
class Person(val name:String, var age:Int)
```

That's it! Another neat example is delegation. Kotlin delegates allow you to provide logic for any number of read operations. One example is the lazy initialization, a concept sure to be familiar to Java developers. It might look like this:

```java
public class SomeClass {
  private SomeHeavyInstance someHeavyInstance = null;
  public SomeHeavyInstance getSomeHeavyInstance() {
    if (someHeavyInstance == null) {
      someHeavyInstance = new SomeHeavyInstance();
    }
    return someHeavyInstance;
  }
}
```

Again, not too terrible, done simply and without configuration, but chances are you'll repeat this same code several times in your code, violating the DRY principle (Don't Repeat Yourself). Also, not thread-safe. Here's the Kotlin version:

```kotlin
val someHeavyInstance by lazy {
  return SomeHeavyInstance()
}
```

Short and sweet and readable. All that boilerplate is tucked away nicely under the covers. Oh, and it's thread-safe too. null safety is also a big upgrade. You'll see a lot of question mark operators following a nullable reference in Kotlin:

```kotlin
val something = someObject?.someMember?.anotherMember
```

Here's the same thing in Java:

```java
Object something = null;
if (someObject != null) {
  if (someObject.someMember != null) {
    if (someObject.someMember.anotherMember != null) {
      something = someObject.someMember.anotherMember;
    }
  }
}
```

The null-check operator (?) will stop evaluating immediately and return null as soon as any of the referents in the chain resolve to null.

Let's close out with another killer feature: coroutines. In a nutshell, a coroutine performs work asynchronous to the calling code, although that work may be handed off to some number of threads. It's important to note that even if a single thread handles multiple coroutines, Kotlin performs some context-switching magic that runs multiple jobs concurrently. While specific behavior is configurable, coroutines naturally use a dedicated thread pool, but use context switching within a single thread (so hot). Since they're Kotlin, they also can be fancy and sophisticated and overengineered, but by default they're also super simple:

```kotlin
launch {
  println("Hi from another context")
}
```

Be aware of the differences between threads and coroutines though—for example, an object.wait() invocation in one job will pause all the other jobs working in the containing thread. Give Kotlin a spin and see what you think.

Learn Java Idioms and Cache in Your Brain

Jeanne Boyarsky

As programmers, there are some tasks we need to do frequently. For example, going through data and applying a condition are common. Here are two ways to count how many positive numbers are in a list:

```java
public int loopImplementation(int[] nums) {
  int count = 0;
  for (int num : nums) {
    if (num > 0) {
      count++;
    }
  }
  return count;
}

public long streamImplementation(int[] nums) {
  return Arrays.stream(nums)
               .filter(n -> n > 0)
               .count();
}
```

Both of these accomplish the same thing, and they both use common Java idioms. An idiom is a common way of expressing some small piece of functionality that the community has general agreement on. Knowing how to write these quickly without having to think about them enables you to write code much faster. As you write code, look for patterns like these. You can even practice them to get faster and learn them by heart.

Some idioms, like looping, conditions, and streams, apply to all Java programmers. Others are more specific to the types of code you work on. For example, I do a lot with regular expressions and file I/O. The following idiom is one I commonly use in file I/O. It reads a file, removes any blank lines, and writes it back:

```
Path path = Paths.get("words.txt");
List<String> lines = Files.readAllLines(path);
lines.removeIf(t -> t.trim().isEmpty());
Files.write(path, lines);
```

If I were on a team where files didn't fit in memory, I'd have to use a different programming idiom. However, I deal with small files where this is not an issue, so the convenience of four lines to do something powerful is worth it.

Notice with these idioms that much of the code is common regardless of your task. If I want to get negative numbers or odd numbers, I just change the if statement or filter. If I want to remove all lines that are more than 60 characters long, I just change the condition in removeIf:

```
lines.removeIf(t -> t.length() <= 60);
```

Regardless, I'm thinking about what I want to accomplish. I'm not looking up how to read a file or how to count values. That's an idiom I learned long ago.

An interesting thing about idioms is that you don't always learn them intentionally. I never sat down and decided to learn the idiom for reading/writing a file. I learned it from using it a lot. Looking up information repeatedly helps you learn it. Or at least helps you know where to find it. For example, I have trouble remembering the regular expression flags. I know what they do, but mix up ?s and ?m. I have looked it up enough times that I know I should google "javadoc pattern" to get the answer.

In conclusion, let your brain serve as a cache. Learn the idioms and common library API calls. Know where to look up the rest quickly. This will free you up to let your brain work on the hard stuff!

Learn to Kata and Kata to Learn

Donald Raab

Every Java developer needs to learn new skills and keep their existing skills sharp. The Java ecosystem is enormous and continues to evolve. With so much to learn, the prospect of keeping up may seem daunting. We can help each other keep up in this rapidly changing space if we work together as a community, sharing knowledge and practice. Taking, creating, and sharing code katas is one of the ways we can do this.

A code kata is a hands-on programming exercise that helps you hone specific skills through practice. Some code katas will provide you structure to validate that a skill has been acquired by getting unit tests to pass. Code katas are a great way for developers to share practice exercises with their future selves and other developers to learn from.

Here's how to create your first code kata:

1. Select a topic you want to learn.

2. Write a passing unit test that demonstrates some piece of knowledge.

3. Refactor the code repeatedly until you are satisfied with the final solution. Make sure the test passes after each refactoring.

4. Delete the solution in the exercise and leave a failing test.

5. Commit the failing test with supporting code and build artifacts to a version control system (VCS).

6. Open source the code to share with others.

Now I'll demonstrate how to create a small kata by following the first four steps:

1. Topic: Learn how to join strings in a List.

2. Write a passing JUnit test that shows how to join strings in a List:

```
@Test
public void joinStrings() {
    List<String> names = Arrays.asList("Sally", "Ted", "Mary");
    StringBuilder builder = new StringBuilder();
    for (int i = 0; i < names.size(); i++) {
      if (i > 0) {
          builder.append(", "); }
          builder.append(names.get(i));
      }
      String joined = builder.toString();
      Assert.assertEquals("Sally, Ted, Mary", joined);
}
```

3. Refactor the code to use StringJoiner in Java 8. Rerun the test:

```
StringJoiner joiner = new StringJoiner(", ");
for (String name : names) {
    joiner.add(name);
}
String joined = joiner.toString();
```

Refactor the code to use Java 8 streams. Rerun the test:

```
String joined = names.stream().collect(Collectors.joining(", "));
```

Refactor the code to use String.join. Rerun the test:

```
String joined = String.join(", ", names);
```

4. Delete the solution and leave a failing test with a comment:

```
@Test
public void joinStrings() {
    List<String> names = Arrays.asList("Sally", "Ted", "Mary");
    // Join the names and separate them by ", "
    String joined = null;
    Assert.assertEquals("Sally, Ted, Mary", joined);
}
```

Pay it forward—I'll leave steps 5 and 6 as an exercise for the reader.

This example should be simple enough to illustrate how to create your own katas of varying complexity, leveraging unit tests to provide the structure necessary to build confidence and understanding.

Value your own learning and knowledge. When you learn something useful, write it down. Saving practice exercises to recall how things work can be quite helpful. Capture your knowledge and exploration in code katas. Katas you have used to sharpen your own skills may also be valuable to others.

We all have things to learn and that we can teach. When we share what we learn with others, we improve the whole Java community. This is vitally important to helping ourselves and our fellow Java developers collectively improve our coding skills.

Learn to Love Your Legacy Code

Uberto Barbini

What is a legacy system? It is old software that is very hard to maintain, to extend, and to improve. On the other hand, it is also a system that is working and is serving the business; otherwise, it would not have survived.

Perhaps, when it was first created, a legacy system had an excellent design, a design so good that people started to say, "OK, maybe we can use it also for this, and this, and this." It becomes overloaded with technical debt, but it still works. These systems can be amazingly resilient.

Still, developers hate working on legacy systems. It can seem there's more technical debt than anybody could ever repay. Perhaps we should just declare bankruptcy and move on. Much easier.

What if you really have to maintain it? What do you do when you have to fix a bug?

Solution number one: duct tape. Hold your nose, fix the defect—"OK, we may regret this one day, but let's do this copy–paste now, just to fix it." From there it will only get worse. Like in an abandoned building, it may stay undamaged for a long time, but as soon as there is a single broken window, it will soon be left without any windows intact. Just seeing one broken window encourages people to break others. This is the law of broken windows.

Solution number two: forget the old system and rewrite from scratch. Can you imagine what the problem with this solution is? More often than not, the rewrite will not work or it will never be finished. This comes from survival bias (*https://oreil.ly/lKSDd*). You see the old system code and say, "Oh, come on, if whoever wrote this terrible code was able to make it work, it must be quite easy." But it's not. You may consider the code horrible, but it's code that has already survived many battles. When you start from scratch, you don't know the battle stories, and you've lost a lot of knowledge about the domain.

So what should we do? In Japan, there is an art called *kintsugi* (*https://oreil.ly/F4AZX*). When a precious object breaks, instead of throwing it away, it is put back together using gold powder along its cracking lines. The gold emphasizes that it was broken, but it's still beautiful.

Perhaps we are looking at the legacy code from the wrong point of view? I am not saying we should goldplate the old code, but we should learn how to fix it in a way that makes us proud of it.

The strangler pattern (*https://oreil.ly/SWJFc*) allows us to do precisely this. It is named for a fig tree (*https://oreil.ly/jficR*) (not for homicide!) that wraps around other trees. Its growth progressively surrounds the host tree, which withers away until all that is left are the fig vines around a hollow core.

Similarly, we start replacing a smelly line of code with a new, clean one that has been thoroughly tested. And then, proceeding from there, we create a new application that creeps on top of the previous one until it completely replaces the old one.

But even if we don't complete it, the mix of new and old is much better than letting the old one rot. It is much safer than a complete rewrite because we will validate the new behavior continuously, and we can always roll back the latest version in case we introduced bugs.

Legacy code deserves a little love.

Learn to Use New Java Features

Gail C. Anderson

Java 8 introduced lambdas and streams, two game-changing features that give Java programmers significant language constructs. From Java 9 onward, release cycles occur every six months with more features popping up in each release. You should care about these new features because they help you write better code. And, your skills will improve as you incorporate new language paradigms into your programming arsenal.

Much has been written about streams and how they support a functional programming style, reduce bulky code, and make code more readable. So, let's look at an example with streams, not so much to convince you to use streams everywhere but to entice you to learn about this and other Java features introduced since Java 8.

Our example computes the maximum, average, and minimum for systolic, diastolic, and pulse values from collected blood-pressure monitoring data. We want to visualize these computed summary statistics with a JavaFX bar chart.

Here's a portion of our `BPData` model class, showing just the getter methods we need:

```
public class BPData {
  ...
  public final Integer getSystolic() {
    return systolic.get();
  }
  public final Integer getDiastolic() {
    return diastolic.get();
  }
  public final Integer getPulse() {
    return pulse.get();
```

```
        }
        ...
}
```

The JavaFX bar chart creates the magic for this visualization. First, we need to build the correct series and feed our transformed data to the bar chart object. Since the operation is repeated for each series, it makes sense to create a single method to parameterize both the bar chart series and the specific BPData getter required to access this data. Our source data is stored in the variable sortedList, a date-sorted collection of BPData elements. Here's the computeStatData method that builds our chart data:

```java
private void computeStatData(
        XYChart.Series<String, Number> targetList,
        Function<BPData, Integer> f) {
    // Set Maximum
    targetList.getData().get(MAX).setYValue(sortedList.stream()
        .mapToInt(f::apply)
        .max()
        .orElse(1));
    // Set Average
    targetList.getData().get(AVG).setYValue(sortedList.stream()
        .mapToInt(f::apply)
        .average()
        .orElse(1.0));
    // Set Minimum
    targetList.getData().get(MIN).setYValue(sortedList.stream()
        .mapToInt(f::apply)
        .min()
        .orElse(1));
}
```

Parameter targetList is the bar chart series data that corresponds to one of systolic, diastolic, or pulse data. We want to create a bar chart with the maximum, average, and minimum corresponding to each of these series. Thus, we set the chart's Y-value to these computed values. The second parameter is the specific getter from BPData, passed as a method reference. We use this in the stream mapToInt method to access the specific values for that series. Each stream sequence returns the maximum, average, or minimum of the source data. Each terminating stream method returns orElse, an Optional object, making our bar chart display a placeholder value of 1 (or 1.0) if the source data stream is empty.

Here's how to invoke this `computeStatData` method. The convenient method reference notation makes it easy to specify which `BPData` getter method to invoke for each data series:

```
computeStatData(systolicStats, BPData::getSystolic);
computeStatData(diastolicStats, BPData::getDiastolic);
computeStatData(pulseStats, BPData::getPulse);
```

Prior to Java 8, this code was much more tedious to write. So, learning and using new Java features is a worthwhile skill to embrace as Java continues to improve.

For your next feature, how about checking out Java 14's `record` syntax, a preview feature, to simplify the `BPData` class?

Learn Your IDE to Reduce Cognitive Load

Trisha Gee

I work for a firm that sells IDEs, so of course I'm going to say you should know how your IDE works and use it properly. Before that, I spent 15 years working with multiple IDEs, learning how they help developers create something useful and how to use them to easily automate tasks.

We all know IDEs provide code highlighting and show errors and potential problems, but any Java IDE can do so much more than that. Learning what your IDE is capable of and using the features that apply to your daily work can help level up your productivity.

For example, your IDE:

- Can generate code for you so you don't have to type it. Getters and setters, `equals` and `hashCode`, and `toString` are the most frequent examples.

- Has refactoring tools that can automatically move your code in a particular direction while keeping the compiler happy.

- Can run your tests and help you debug problems. If you're using `System.out` for debugging, it's going to take you much longer than if you're inspecting the values of objects at runtime.

- Should integrate with your build and dependency management system so your development environment works the same way as your testing and production environments.

- Can even help you with tools or systems external to your application code—for example, version control, database access, or code review (remember, the *I* in *IDE* stands for *integrated*). You don't have to leave the tool to work with all aspects of your software delivery pipeline.

Using the IDE, you can navigate through the code naturally—finding the methods that call this piece of code, or moving into the method that this code calls. You can move directly to files (or even to specific code snippets) using a few keystrokes instead of the mouse to navigate a file structure.

The tool you choose to write code in should be helping you focus on what you're developing. You shouldn't be thinking about the intricacies of how you code it. By offloading the tedious stuff onto the IDE, you reduce your cognitive load and can spend more brain power on the business problem you're trying to solve.

Let's Make a Contract: The Art of Designing a Java API

Mario Fusco

An API is what developers use to achieve some task. More precisely, it establishes a contract between them and the designers of the software, exposing its services through that API. In this sense, we're all API designers: our software doesn't work in isolation but becomes useful only when it interacts with other software written by other developers. When writing software, we're not only consumers but also providers of one or more APIs, which is why every developer should know the characteristics of good APIs and how to achieve them.

Firstly, a good API should be easily understandable and discoverable. It should be possible to start using it and, ideally, learn how it works without reading its documentation. To this end, it's important to use consistent naming and conventions. This sounds pretty obvious; nevertheless, it's easy to find, even in the standard Java API, situations where this suggestion hasn't been followed. For instance, since you can invoke `skip(n)` to skip the first *n* items of a Stream, what could be a good name for the method that skips all the Stream's items until one of them doesn't satisfy a predicate p? A reasonable name could be `skipWhile(p)`, but actually this method is called `drop While(p)`. There's nothing wrong with the name `dropWhile` per se, but it isn't consistent with `skip` performing a very similar operation. Don't do this.

Keeping your API minimal is another way to make it easy to use. This reduces both the concepts to be learned and its maintenance costs. Once again, you can find examples breaking this simple principle in the standard Java API. `Optional` has a `static` factory method `of(object)` that creates an `Optional` wrapping the object passed to it. Incidentally, using factory methods instead of constructors is another valuable practice since it allows greater flexibility: doing so, you can also return an instance of a subclass or even a null when the method is called with illegal arguments. Unfortunately, `Optional.of` throws a `NullPointerException` when invoked with `null`, something unexpected from a class designed to prevent `NullPointerExcep` `tions` (NPEs). This not only breaks the principle of least astonishment—another thing to consider when designing your API—but requires the introduction of a second method `ofNullable` returning an empty `Optional` when called with `null`. The `of` method has an inconsistent behavior and, if implemented correctly, the `ofNullable` one could have been left out.

Other good hints that could improve your API are: break apart large interfaces into smaller pieces; consider implementing a fluent API, for which, this time, Java Streams is a very good example; never return `null`, use empty collections and `Optional` instead; limit usage of exceptions, and possibly avoid checked ones. Regarding method arguments: avoid long lists of them, especially of the same type; use the weakest possible type; keep them in consistent order among different overloads; consider varargs. Moreover, the fact that a good API is self-explanatory doesn't mean that you shouldn't document it clearly and extensively.

Finally, don't expect to write a great API the first time. Designing an API is an iterative process, and dogfooding is the only way to validate and improve it. Write tests and examples against your API and discuss them with colleagues and users. Iterate multiple times to eliminate unclear intentions, redundant code, and leaky abstraction.

Make Code Simple and Readable

Emily Jiang

I am a big fan of simple and readable code. Every line of code should be as self-explanatory as possible. Every line of code should be necessary. To achieve readable and simple code, there are two aspects: format and content. Here are some tips to help you write code that is readable and simple:

Use indentation to lay out your code clearly.
Use it consistently. If you work in a project, there should be a code template. Everyone on the team should adopt the same code format. Don't mix spaces with tabs. I always have the IDE configured to display spaces and tabs so that I can spot the mix and fix them. (Personally, I love spaces.) Choose either spaces or tabs, and stick to it.

Use meaningful variable names and method names.
The code is much easier to maintain if it is self-explanatory. With meaningful identifiers, your code can talk for itself instead of needing a separate comment line to explain what it does. Steer clear of single-letter variable names. If your variable and method names have clear meaning, you will not normally need comments to explain what your code does.

Comment your code if necessary.
If the logic is very complex, such as regex queries, etc., use documentation to explain what the code is trying to do. Once there are comments, you need to ensure they are maintained. Unmaintained comments cause confusion. If you need to warn a maintainer about something, make sure you document it and make it stand out, such as adding "WARNING" at the start of a comment. Sometimes a bug can be spotted and fixed more easily if the original author expresses their intention or puts a warning somewhere.

Don't check in commented-out code.

Delete it to improve the readability. One of the common arguments for the commented-out code is that some day the commented-out code might be needed. The truth is that it might stay there for years, unmaintained and causing confusion. Even if one day you want to uncomment it, the code block might not compile or work as expected as the base might have changed significantly. Don't hesitate. Just delete it.

Don't overengineer by adding might-be-useful-in-the-future code.

If you are tasked to deliver some functionality, don't overdo it by including additional speculative logic. Any extra code runs the risk of introducing bugs and maintenance overhead.

Avoid writing verbose code.

Aim to write fewer lines of code to achieve a task. More lines introduce more bugs. Prototype first via brainstorming to get the task done, and then polish the code. Make sure each line has a strong reason to exist. If you are a manager or architect, don't judge your developers by how many lines of code they deliver but by how clean and readable their code is.

Learn functional programming, if you have not already.

One of the advantages of using features introduced in Java 8, such as lambdas and streams, is that these features can help to improve your code readability.

Adopt pair programming.

Pair programming is a great way for a junior developer to learn from someone who is more experienced. It is also a great way to write meaningful code, as you need to explain your choices and reasoning to the other person. A great process encourages you to write code with care instead of dumping code.

Code will have fewer bugs if it is simple and readable: code that is complex is likely to have more bugs; code that is not easily understood is likely to have more bugs. Hopefully, these tips can help you to improve your skills and your code, to deliver code that is simple and readable!

Make Your Java Groovier

Ken Kousen

The screen was the color of a cyberpunk novel opened to the first line. I stared at it, worried I would never finish tonight. There was a knock on the wall of my cubicle. My boss stood there, waiting.

"How's it going?" she said.

"Java is so verbose," I sighed. "I just want to download some data from a service and save it to a database. I'm swimming in builders, factories, library code, try/catch blocks..."

"Just add Groovy."

"Huh? How would that help?"

She sat down. "Mind if I drive?"

"Please."

"Let me give you a quick demo." She opened a command prompt and typed groovyConsole. A simple GUI appeared on the screen. "Say you want to know how many astronauts are in space at the moment. There's a service at Open Notify (*https://oreil.ly/oysGk*) that gives you that."

She executed the following in the Groovy console:

```
def jsonTxt = 'http://api.open-notify.org/astros.json'.toURL().text
```

The JSON response came back with the number of astronauts, a status message, and nested objects relating each astronaut to a craft.

"Groovy adds toURL to String to generate a java.net.URL, and getText to URL to retrieve the data, which you access as text."

"Sweet," I said. "Now I have to map that to Java classes and use a library like Gson or Jackson—"

"Nah. If all you want is the number of people in space, just use a Json Slurper."

"A what?"

She typed:

```
def number = new JsonSlurper().parseText(jsonTxt).number
```

"The `parseText` method returns `Object`," she said, "but we don't care about the type here, so just drill down."

It turned out there were six people in space, all aboard the International Space Station.

"OK," I said. "Say I want to parse the response into classes. What then? Is there a port of Gson to Groovy?"

She shook her head. "Don't need it. It's all bytecodes under the hood. Just instantiate the `Gson` class and invoke methods as usual:

```
@Canonical
class Assignment { String name; String craft }
@Canonical
class Response { String message; int number; Assignment[] people }
new Gson().fromJson(jsonTxt, Response).people.each { println it }
```

"The `Canonical` annotation adds `toString`, `equals`, `hashCode`, a default constructor, a named argument constructor, and a tuple constructor to each class."

"Awesome! Now how do I save the astronauts in a database?"

"Easy enough. Let's use H2 for this sample:

```
Sql sql = Sql.newInstance(url: 'jdbc:h2:~/astro',
                          driver: 'org.h2.Driver')
sql.execute '''
 create table if not exists ASTRONAUTS(
   id int auto_increment primary key,
   name varchar(50),
   craft varchar(50)
 )
 '''
response.people.each {
 sql.execute "insert into ASTRONAUTS(name, craft)" +
             "values ($it.name, $it.craft)"
}
sql.close()
```

"The Groovy Sql class creates a table using a multiline string and inserts values using interpolated strings:

```
sql.eachRow('select * from ASTRONAUTS') {
  row -> println "${row.name.padRight(20)} aboard ${row.craft}"
}
```

"Done," she said, "with a formatted print and everything."

I stared at the result. "Do you have any idea how many lines of Java that would have been?" I asked.

She smirked. "A lot. By the way, all exceptions in Groovy are unchecked, so you don't even need a try/catch block. If we use withInstance rather than newInstance, the connection will close automatically too. Good enough?"

I nodded.

"Now just wrap the different parts into a class, and you can call it from Java."

She left, and I looked forward to making the rest of my Java groovier.

Minimal Constructors

Steve Freeman

A pattern I regularly see is significant work done in the constructor: take in a set of arguments and convert them into values for the fields. It often looks like this:

```
public class Thing {
    private final Fixed fixed;
    private Details details;
    private NotFixed notFixed;
    // more fields

    public Thing(Fixed fixed,
                 Dependencies dependencies,
                 OtherStuff otherStuff) {
        this.fixed = fixed;
        setup(dependencies, otherStuff);
    }
}
```

I assume that setup initializes the remaining fields based on dependencies and otherStuff, but it's not clear to me from the constructor signature exactly what values are necessary to create a new instance. It's also not obvious which fields can change during the life of the object, as they cannot be made final unless they're initialized in a constructor. Finally, this class is harder to unit test than it should be because instantiating it requires creating the right structure in the arguments to be passed to setup.

Worse, I occasionally used to see constructors like this:

```
public class Thing {
    private Weather currentWeather;
    public Thing(String weatherServiceHost) {
        currentWeather = getWeatherFromHost(weatherServiceHost);
```

```
        }
    }
```

which requires an internet connection and a service to create an instance. Thankfully, this is now rare.

All of this was done with the best of intentions to make creating instances easier by "encapsulating" behavior. I believe this approach is a legacy from C++ where programmers can use constructors and destructors creatively to control resources. It's easier to combine classes in an inheritance hierarchy if each manages its own internal dependencies.

I prefer to use an approach inspired by my experience of Modula-3 (*https://oreil.ly/t2t4G*), which is that all a constructor does is assign values to fields: its only job is to create a valid instance. If there's more work to do, I use a factory method:

```java
public class Thing {
    private final Fixed fixed;
    private final Details details;
    private NotFixed notFixed;

    public Thing(Fixed fixed, Details details, NotFixed notFixed) {
        this.fixed = fixed;
        this.details = details;
        this.notFixed = notFixed;
    }

    public static Thing forInternationalShipment(
            Fixed fixed,
            Dependencies dependencies,
            OtherStuff otherStuff) {
        final var intermediate = convertFrom(dependencies, otherStuff);
        return new Thing(fixed,
                        intermediate.details(),
                        intermediate.initialNotFixed());
    }

    public static Thing forLocalShipment(Fixed fixed,
                                         Dependencies dependencies) {
        return new Thing(fixed,
                        localShipmentDetails(dependencies),
                        NotFixed.DEFAULT_VALUE);
```

```
        }
    }

final var internationalShipment =
    Thing.forInternationalShipment(fixed, dependencies, otherStuff);
final var localShipment = Thing.forLocalShipment(fixed, dependencies);
```

The advantages are that:

- I'm now very clear about the life cycle of the instance fields.
- I've separated code for the instantiation of an object from its use.
- The name of the factory method describes itself, unlike a constructor.
- The class and its instantiation are easier to unit test separately.

There is a disadvantage around not being able to share constructor implementation in inheritance hierarchies, but that can be addressed by making the supporting helper methods accessible and, more usefully, by taking the hint to avoid deep inheritance.

Finally, to me, this is also a reason to be careful about how to work with dependency injection frameworks. If creating an object is complicated, then putting everything in the constructor because that makes reflection-based tooling easier to use feels backward to me. One can usually register the factory method instead as a way to create new instances. Similarly, using reflection to set private fields directly for "encapsulation" (or to avoid writing a constructor) breaks the type system and makes unit testing more difficult; it's better to set the fields through a minimal constructor. Use @Inject or @Autowired cautiously and make everything explicit.

Name the Date

Kevlin Henney

As `java.util.Date` is slowly but surely deprecated into the Sun-set, with `java.time` taking up its mantle, it's worth pausing to learn some lessons from its troubled life before letting it rest in peace.

The most obvious lesson is that date–time handling is harder than people expect—even when they're expecting it. It is a truth universally acknowledged that a single programmer in possession of the belief they understand dates and times must be in want of a code review. But that's not what I want to focus on here, nor is it the importance of immutability for value types, what makes a class (un)suitable for subclassing, or how to use classes rather than integers to express a rich domain.

Source code is made up of spacing, punctuation, and names. All these convey meaning to the reader, but names are where most meaning is carried (or dropped). Names matter. A lot.

Given its name, it would be nice if a `Date` represented a calendar date, i.e., a specific day...but it doesn't. It represents a point in time that can be viewed as having a date component. This is more commonly referred to as a *date–time* or, if you want to put it into code, a `DateTime`. `Time` also works, as it is the overarching concept. Sometimes finding the right name is hard; in this case it's not.

Now we understand what we mean by date, date–time, and `Date`, what does `getDate` do? Does it return the whole date–time value? Or perhaps just the date component? Neither: it returns the day of the month. In programming circles, this value is more commonly and specifically referred to as *day of month*, not *date*, a term normally reserved for representing a calendar date.

And while we're here, yes, `getDay` would have been better named `getDayOf Week`. Not only is it important to choose a name that is correct but it is important to recognize and resolve ambiguous terms such as *day* (of week, of month, of year...?). Note that it is better to resolve naming issues by choosing a better name rather than by Javadoc.

Names are tied to conventions, and conventions are tied to names. When it comes to conventions, prefer one (not many), prefer to express it clearly, and prefer one that is widely recognized and easy to use rather than one that is niche and error-prone (yeah, C, I'm looking at you).

For example, Apollo 11 landed on the moon at 20:17 on the twentieth day of July (the seventh month) in 1969 (CE, UTC, etc.). But if you call `getTime`, `getDate`, `getMonth`, and `getYear` expecting these numbers, expect disappointment: `getTime` returns a negative number of milliseconds from the start of 1970; `getDate` returns 20 (as expected, it counts from 1); `getMonth` returns 6 (months count from 0); and `getYear` returns 69 (years count from 1900, not 0 and not 1970).

Good naming is part of design. It sets expectations and communicates a model, showing how something should be understood and used. If you mean to tell the reader `getMillisSince1970`, don't say `getTime`. Specific names inspire you to consider alternatives, to question whether you're capturing the right abstraction in the right way. It's not just labeling, and it's not just `java.util.Date`: this is about the code you write and the code you use.

The Necessity of Industrial-Strength Technologies

Paul W. Homer

Java may have been called the next COBOL, but that's not necessarily a bad thing.

COBOL has been an incredibly successful technology. Reliable, consistent, and easy to read, it has been the workhorse of the Information Age, managing the bulk of the world's mission-critical systems. If the syntax requires lots of extra typing, that is offset by the sheer number of readers that have had to ponder its behavior.

Trendy software stacks sound cool—and, as most are quite immature, there is always plenty to learn—but the world needs reliable industrial-strength software to function. A new clever idiom or slightly obfuscated paradigm can be great fun to play with, but by definition they are shrouded in unknowns. We're obsessed with finding some magical way to just snap our fingers and will the next enterprise-class system into existence, but we keep forgetting that over three decades ago Frederick Brooks Jr. said those kinds of magic bullets—silver or otherwise—just can't exist.

We don't need the next trendy toy to solve real problems for people. We need to put in the thinking and the work to fully understand and codify reliable solutions. Systems that only work on sunny days, or that need to be rewritten every year or so, don't satisfy our growing needs for managing the complexities of modern society. It doesn't matter how it works if it is unpredictable when it fails. Instead, we have to fully encapsulate our knowledge into reliable, reusable, recomposable components, leveraging them for as long as possible to keep up with the chaotic nature of our current period in history. If the code doesn't last, it probably wasn't worth writing.

Java is a great technology for this purpose: new enough to contain modern language features, but mature enough to be trustworthy. We've gotten better at organizing large codebases well, and there is a great enough wealth of supporting products, tools, and ecosystems to shift the focus back to real business problems and away from the purely technical ones. It's a strong stack for decoupling the systems from their environments, yet standard enough to find experienced staff. If it isn't the talk of the town, it is at least a very reliable, stable platform on which to build systems that last for decades, and that, it seems, is what we both want and need for our current development efforts.

Fashion should not dictate engineering. Software development is a discipline of knowledge and organization. If you don't know how the parts will behave, you can't ensure that the whole will behave. If the solution is unreliable, then it really just adds to the problem rather than solving it. It may be fun just to toss together some code that kinda works, but it is only professional if we build stuff that can withstand reality and keep humming along.

Only Build the Parts
That Change and
Reuse the Rest

Jenn Strater

As Java programmers, we spend a lot of time waiting for builds to run, often because we don't run them efficiently. We can make small improvements by changing our behavior. For example, we could only run a submodule instead of the entire project, and not run clean before every build. To make a bigger difference, we should take advantage of the build caching offered by our build tools, namely Gradle, Maven, and Bazel.

Build caching is the reuse of results from a previous run to minimize the number of build steps (e.g., Gradle tasks, Maven goals, Bazel actions) executed during the current run. Any build step that is idempotent, meaning that it produces the same output for a given set of inputs, can be cached.

The output of Java compilation, for example, is the tree of class files generated by the Java compiler, and the inputs are factors that impact the produced class files, such as the source code itself, Java version, operating system, and any compiler flags. Given the same run conditions and source code, the Java compilation step produces the same class files every time. So instead of running the compilation step, the build tool can look in the cache for any previous runs with the same inputs and reuse the output.

Build caching isn't limited to compilation. Build tools define standard inputs and outputs for other common build steps, like static analysis and documentation generation, and also allow us to configure the inputs and outputs for any cacheable build step.

This type of caching is especially useful for multimodule builds. In a project with 4 modules, each of which has 5 build steps, a clean build must execute 20 steps. Most of the time, though, we are only modifying the source code in one module. If no other projects depend on that module, then that means we only need to execute the steps downstream from source code generation; in this example, only 4: the outputs of the other 16 steps can be pulled from the cache, saving time and resources.

Gradle's incremental build, which we see as UP-TO-DATE in the build output, implements build caching at the project level. A local cache, like the one built into Gradle and available as an extension to Maven, works even when changing workspaces, Git branches, and command-line options.

The collaborative effect of remote build caching available in Gradle, Maven, and Bazel adds additional benefits. One of the common use cases for remote caching is the first build after pulling from a remote version control repository. After we pull from the remote, we have to build the project on our machine to take advantage of those changes. But since we have never built those changes on our machine, they aren't in our local cache yet. However, the continuous integration system has already built those changes and uploaded the results to the shared remote cache so we get a cache hit from the remote cache, saving the time required to execute those build steps locally.

By using build caching in our Java builds, we can share the results across our local builds, the agents of the CI server, and the entire team, resulting in faster builds for everyone and fewer resources computing the same operations over and over again.

Open Source Projects Aren't Magic

Jenn Strater

One of my biggest pet peeves is hearing people say that X technology, language, build tool, etc., works by magic. If that project is open source, then what I hear is "I'm too lazy to look up how it works," and I'm reminded of Clarke's Third Law that "any sufficiently advanced technology is indistinguishable from magic."[1]

In the days of the modern web, it is easier than ever before to look up the reference guides and source code and find out how that technology works. Many open source projects like the Apache Groovy programming language, for example, have a website (in this case, groovy-lang.org (*https://groovy-lang.org*)) that lists where you can find the documentation, reference guides, bug tracker, and even links to the source code itself.

If you're looking for help getting started, guides and tutorials are a great place to begin. If you are more of a visual or hands-on learner, many online learning platforms offer introductory courses for learning new languages through labs, exercises, and group work. Sometimes these are even freely available so that the technologies will be more widely known.

After learning the basic syntax and data structures and starting to use them in your own projects, you'll likely start encountering unexpected behaviors or even bugs. No matter which ecosystem you choose, this will happen at some point. It's just a part of the world we live in. You should first look for an issue tracker like Jira or GitHub issues to see if others are having the same problem. If so, there may be workarounds, a fix in a newer version, or a timeline for when this issue will be fixed.

---

1 Arthur C. Clarke, *Profiles of the Future: An Inquiry into the Limits of the Possible.* (London: Pan Books, 1973). Now, yes, there is a formal definition in computer science that refers to hiding the implementation details through abstraction, but most people misuse the term "magic" to describe any technology that they find difficult to understand.

It may take a little work to find out where your technology's community collaborates. Sometimes it is in chat rooms, forums, or mailing lists. Projects in the Apache foundation, in particular, tend to use Apache infrastructure rather than commercial products. Finding this place is the best way to move from "magic" to clarity.

Even after you master a particular technology, learning is a continuous process and you'll need to keep doing it. New releases may add new features or change behaviors in ways you will need to understand. Join the mailing list or attend conferences with the open source committers to learn what you need for upgrading your projects. If you are already a subject matter expert, this is a great way you can also contribute to uncovering the "magic" for everyone else.

Lastly, if you find something is unclear or missing, many projects are happy to accept contributions, especially to documentation. The project leads are often people with regular day jobs and other priorities, so they may not respond right away, but this is the best way to help everyone succeed and to uncover the "magic" for the next generation of users.

Optional Is a Lawbreaking Monad but a Good Type

Nicolai Parlog

In most programming languages, empty-or-not-empty types are well-behaved monads. (Yes, I used the M-word—don't worry, no math.) This means their mechanics fulfill a couple of definitions and follow a number of laws that guarantee safe (de)composition of computations.

Optional's methods fulfill these definitions *but* break the laws. Not without consequences...

Monad Definition

You need three things to define a monad—in Optional's terms:

1. The type Optional<T> itself

2. The method ofNullable(T) that wraps a value T into an Optional<T>

3. The method flatMap(Function<T, Optional<U>>) that applies the given function to the value that is wrapped by the Optional on which it is called

There's an alternative definition using map instead of flatMap, but it's too long to fit here.

Monad Laws

Now it gets interesting—a monad has to fulfill three laws to be one of the cool kids. In Optional's terms:

1. For a Function<T, Optional<U>> f and a value v, f.apply(v) must equal Optional.ofNullable(v).flatMap(f). This *left identity* guarantees it doesn't matter whether you apply a function directly or let Optional do it.

2. Calling `flatMap(Optional::ofNullable)` returns an `Optional` that equals the one you called it on. This *right identity* guarantees applying no-ops doesn't change anything.

3. For an `Optional<T>` o and two functions `Function<T, Optional<U>> f` and `Function<U, Optional<V>> g`, the results of `o.flatMap(f).flat` `Map(g)` and `o.flatMap(v -> f.apply(v).flatMap(g))` must be equal. This *associativity* guarantees that it doesn't matter whether functions are flat-mapped individually or as a composition.

While `Optional` holds up in most cases, it doesn't for a specific edge case. Have a look at `flatMap`'s implementation:

```
public <U> Optional<U> flatMap(Function<T, Optional<U>> f) {
    if (!isPresent()) {
        return empty();
    } else {
        return f.apply(this.value);
    }
}
```

You can see that it doesn't apply the function to an empty `Optional`, which makes it easy to break left identity:

```
Function<Integer, Optional<String>> f =
    i -> Optional.of(i == null ? "NaN" : i.toString());
// the following are not equal
Optional<String> containsNaN = f.apply(null);
Optional<String> isEmpty = Optional.ofNullable(null).flatMap(f);
```

That's not great, but it's even worse for `map`. Here, associativity means that given an `Optional<T>` o and two functions `Function<T, U> f` and `Func` `tion<U, V> g`, the results of `o.map(f).map(g)` and `o.map(f.andThen(g))` must be equal:

```
Function<Integer, Integer> f = i -> i == 0 ? null : i;
Function<Integer, String> g = i -> i == null ? "NaN" : i.toString();
// the following are not equal
Optional<String> containsNaN = Optional.of(0).map(f.andThen(g));
Optional<String> isEmpty = Optional.of(0).map(f).map(g);
```

So What?

The examples may seem contrived and the importance of the laws unclear, but the impact is real: in an Optional chain, you can't mechanically merge and split operations because that may change the code's behavior. That is unfortunate because proper monads let you ignore them when you want to focus on readability or domain logic.

But why is Optional a broken monad? *Because* null-*safety is more important!* To uphold the laws, an Optional would have to be able to contain null while being nonempty. And it would have to pass it to functions given to map and flatMap. Imagine if everything you did in map and flatMap had to check for null! *That* Optional would be a great monad, but provide zero null-safety.

No, I'm happy we got the Optional that we got.

Package-by-Feature with the Default Access Modifier

Marco Beelen

A lot of business applications are written using a three-tier architecture: view, business, and data layers, and all model objects are used by all three layers.

In some codebases, the classes for these applications are organized by layer. In some applications, which have the need to register various users and the company they work for, the code structure would result in something like:

```
tld.domain.project.model.Company
tld.domain.project.model.User
tld.domain.project.controllers.CompanyController
tld.domain.project.controllers.UserController
tld.domain.project.storage.CompanyRepository
tld.domain.project.storage.UserRepository
tld.domain.project.service.CompanyService
tld.domain.project.service.UserService
```

Using such a *package-by-layer* structure for your classes requires a lot of methods to be public. The UserService needs to be able to read and write Users into storage and, since the UserRepository is in another package, almost all methods of the UserRepository would need to be public.

The organization might have a policy to send an email to a user to notify them when their password has been changed. Such a policy might be implemented in the UserService. Since the methods in the UserRepository are public, there is no protection against another part of the application invoking a method in UserRepository, which changes the password but does not trigger the notification to be sent.

When this application is updated to include some customer-care module or a web-care interface, some of the features in those modules might want to reset the password. Since these features are built at a later point in time, perhaps after new developers have joined the team, these developers might be tempted to access the UserRepository directly from a CustomerCareService instead of calling the UserService and triggering the notification.

The Java language provides a mechanism to prevent this: access modifiers.

The default access modifier means we do not explicitly declare an access modifier for a class, field, method, etc. A variable or method declared without any access control modifier is available only to other classes in the same package. This is also called *package-private*.

In order to benefit from that access protection mechanism, the code base should be organized into a *package-by-feature* package hierarchy.

The same classes as before would be packaged like this:

```
tld.domain.project.company.Company
tld.domain.project.company.CompanyController
tld.domain.project.company.CompanyService
tld.domain.project.company.CompanyRepository
tld.domain.project.user.User
tld.domain.project.user.UserController
tld.domain.project.user.UserService
tld.domain.project.user.UserRepository
```

When organized like this, none of the methods in the UserRepository would have to be public. They all could be *package-private* and still be available to the UserService. The methods of the UserService could be made public.

Any developer building the CustomerCareService, in the package tld.domain.project.support, would not be able to invoke methods on the UserRepository and should call the methods of the UserService. This way the code structure and the access modifiers help to ensure that the application still adheres to the policy to send the notification.

This strategy for organizing the classes in your codebase will help reduce the coupling in your codebase.

Production Is the Happiest Place on Earth

Josh Long

Production is my first favorite place on the internet. I love production. *You* should love production. Go as early and often as possible. Bring the kids. Bring the family. The weather is amazing. It's the happiest place on Earth. It's better than Disneyland!

Getting there isn't always easy, but trust me: once you get there, you're going to want to stay. It's like Mauritius. You'll *love* it! Here are some tips to make your journey as pleasant as possible:

Take the continuous delivery highway.
There's no faster way to production. Continuous delivery lets you move quickly and consistently from the latest Git commit to production. In a continuous delivery pipeline, code moves automatically from developer to deployment, and every step in between, in one smooth motion. Continuous integration tools like Travis CI or Jenkins help, but try to mine information gleaned while in production. Canary releases are a technique to reduce the risk of introducing a new software version in production by slowly rolling out the change to a small cross-section of users. Continuous delivery tools like Netflix's Spinnaker can automate this sort of nuanced deployment strategy.

Production can be surprising.
Be prepared! Services will fail. Don't leave your clients in the lurch. Specify aggressive client-side timeouts. Service-level agreements (SLAs) dominate a lot of technical discussions. Use service-hedging—a pattern in which multiple idempotent calls to identically configured service instances on discrete nodes are launched and all but the fastest response discarded—to meet SLAs. Failures will happen. Use circuit breakers to explicitly define failure modes and isolate failures. Spring Cloud has an abstraction, Spring Cloud Circuit Breaker, that supports reactive and nonreactive circuits.

In production, nobody can hear your application scream.

Embrace observability from the get-go. Production is a busy place! If everything goes well, you'll have more users and demand than you'll know what to do with. As demand increases, scale. Cloud infrastructure like Cloud Foundry, Heroku, and Kubernetes have long supported horizontal scale out by fronting an ensemble of nodes with a load balancer. This is particularly easy if you're building stateless, 12-Factor-style microservices. This strategy works even if your application monopolizes otherwise precious resources like threads.

Your code shouldn't monopolize threads.

Threads are super expensive. The best solutions to this problem—cooperative multithreading—are about giving signals to the runtime about when it can move work on and off a finite set of actual, operating-system threads. Learn about things like reactive programming as supported by Project Reactor (fairly common on the server side) and Spring Webflux and RxJava (fairly common on Android). If you understand how reactive programming works, it's a natural next step to embrace things like Kotlin's coroutines. Cooperative multithreading lets you multiply the number of users supported or divide infrastructure costs.

Autonomy is a key to success.

Microservices enable small, singly-focused teams, able to release software to production autonomously.

Ninety percent of your application is mundane.

Embrace frameworks like Spring Boot to let you focus on the bottom-line production deliverables, and not on supporting code. Is the Java programming language not your cup of tea—er—coffee? The JVM ecosystem is rich with productive alternatives like Kotlin.

Remove the friction of going to production. Eschew what Amazon CTO Werner Vogels calls "undifferentiated heavy lifting."[1] Clear the path to production and people will want to go early and often. They'll yearn for what has been called Antoine de Saint-Exupéry's "vast and endless seas."

---

1 Divina Paredes, "Amazon CTO: Stop Spending Money on 'Undifferentiated Heavy Lifting,'" (*https://oreil.ly/M0cyS*) *CIO*, June 9, 2013.

Program with GUTs

Kevlin Henney

So you're writing unit tests? Great! Are they any good? To borrow a term from Alistair Cockburn, do you have GUTs? Good unit tests? Or have you landed someone (future you?) with interest-accumulating technical debt in their testbase?

What do I mean by *good*? Good question. Hard question. Worth an answer.

Let's start with names. Reflect what is being tested in the name. Yup, you don't want `test1`, `test2`, and `test3` as your naming scheme. In fact, you don't want `test` in your test names: `@Test` already does that. Tell the reader what you're testing, not that you're testing.

Ah, no, I don't mean name it after the method under test: tell the reader what behavior, property, capability, etc. is under test. If you've got a method `addItem`, you don't want a corresponding `addItemIsOK` test. That's a common test smell. Identify the cases of behavior, and test only one case per test case. Oh, and no, that doesn't mean `addItemSuccess` and `addItemFailure`.

Let me ask you, what's the purpose of your test? To test that "it works"? That's only half the story. The biggest challenge in code is not to determine whether "it works," but to determine what "it works" means. You have the chance to capture that meaning, so try `additionOfItemWithUniqueKeyIsRetained` and `additionOfItemWithExistingKeyFails`.

Because these names are long, and also aren't production code, consider using underscores to improve readability—camel case doesn't scale—so `Addition_of_item_with_unique_key_is_retained`. With JUnit 5 you can use `DisplayNameGenerator.ReplaceUnderscores` with `@DisplayName Generation` to pretty-print as "Addition of item with unique key is retained." You can see that naming as a proposition has a nice property: if the test passes, you have some confidence the proposition might be true; if it fails, the proposition is false.

Which is a good point. Passing tests don't guarantee that the code works. But, for a unit test to be good, the meaning of failure should be clear: it should mean the code doesn't work. Like Dijkstra said, "Program testing can be used to show the presence of bugs, but never to show their absence!"[1]

In practice, this means a unit test shouldn't depend on things that can't be controlled within the test. Filesystem? Network? Database? Asynchronous ordering? You may have influence, but not control. The unit under test shouldn't depend on things that could cause failure when the code is correct.

Also, watch out for overfitting tests. You know the ones: brittle assertions on implementation details rather than required features. You update something —spelling, a magic value, a quality outcome—and tests fail. They fail because the tests were at fault, not the production code.

Oh, and keep your eyes open for underfitting tests too. They're vague, passing at the drop of a hat, even with code that's wildly and obviously wrong. You successfully add your first item. Don't just test the number of items is greater than zero. There's only one right outcome: one item. Many integers are greater than zero; billions are wrong.

Speaking of outcome, you may find many tests follow a simple three-act play: *arrange-act-assert*, aka *given-when-then*. Keeping this in mind helps you focus on the story that the test is trying to tell. Keeps it cohesive, suggests other tests, and helps with the name. Oh, and as we're back on names, you may find names get repetitive. Factor out the repetition. Use it to group tests into inner classes with `@Nested`. So, you could nest `with_unique_key_is_retained` and `with_existing_key_fails` inside `Addition_of_item`.

I hope that's been useful. You're off to revisit some tests? OK, catch you later.

---

1 Edsger W. Dijkstra, "Notes on Structured Programming." In *Structured Programming*, O.-J. Dahl, E.W. Dijkstra, and C.A.R. Hoare, eds. (London and New York: Academic Press, 1972), 6.

Read OpenJDK Daily

Heinz M. Kabutz

OpenJDK consists of millions of lines of Java code. Almost every class violates some "clean code" guidelines. The real world is messy. There is no such thing as "clean code," and we will struggle to even define what that is.

Experienced Java programmers can read code that follows different styles. OpenJDK has over a thousand authors. Even though there is some consistency in the formatting, they code in disparate ways.

For example, consider the `Vector.writeObject` method:

```java
private void writeObject(java.io.ObjectOutputStream s)
        throws java.io.IOException {
    final java.io.ObjectOutputStream.PutField fields = s.putFields();
    final Object[] data;
    synchronized (this) {
        fields.put("capacityIncrement", capacityIncrement);
        fields.put("elementCount", elementCount);
        data = elementData.clone();
    }
    fields.put("elementData", data);
    s.writeFields();
}
```

Why did the programmer mark the local variables `fields` and `data` as `final`? There is no reason why this was necessary. It is a coding style decision. Good programmers can read code equally well, whether the local variables are `final` or not. It does not bother them either way.

Why is `fields.put("elementData", data)` outside of the synchronized block? This may have been due to a premature optimization, wanting to reduce the serial section of code. Or perhaps the programmer was careless? It is easy to want to optimize everything we see, but we need to resist this urge.

Here is another method from the `Spliterator` inside `ArrayList`:

```java
public Spliterator<E> trySplit() {
    int hi = getFence(), lo = index, mid = (lo + hi) >>> 1;
    return (lo >= mid) ? null : // divide range in half unless too small
            new RandomAccessSpliterator<>(this, lo, index = mid);
}
```

This method would definitely raise all sorts of "clean code" warning bells. Those in love with `final` would complain that `hi`, `lo`, and `mid` could be `final`. Yeah, they could. But they are not. In OpenJDK they generally do not mark local variables as `final`.

Why do we have this obscure `(lo + hi) >>> 1`? Could we not rather say `(lo + hi) / 2`? (Answer: it's not exactly the same.)

And why are all three local variables declared on a single line? Is that not violating all that is good and proper?

Turns out, according to research, the number of bugs is in proportion to the lines of code. Spread out your method the way that your university professor asked you to, and you have more lines of code (LOC). And with more LOC, you also end up with more bugs for the same functionality. It can also be that rookie programmers tend to spread their code over many pages. Experts write tight, compact code.

We need to learn to read many different styles of coding, and for that, I recommend OpenJDK. Read the `java.util` classes, `java.io`, and so many others out there.

Really Looking Under the Hood

Rafael Benevides

Java is a complete platform and should be treated that way. In my Java development career, I've met hundreds of developers who are deeply familiar with the language's syntax. They understand lambdas and streams and know every API from String to nio off the top of their heads. But understanding the following would make them more complete professionals:

Garbage collection algorithms
The JVM GC has improved a lot since its first versions. The JVM's ergonomics allow it to automatically adjust to have optimal parameters for the detected environment. A good understanding of what is going on can sometimes improve the JVM performance further.

JVM profilers
JVM tuning is not a guessing game. You should understand how the application is behaving before you make any changes. Knowing how to connect and interpret the profiler's data will help you tune the JVM for better performance, find memory leaks, or understand why a method is taking so long to execute.

Cloud-native applications make it clear that code can be executed on multiple machines across a network over different operating systems. Knowing the following can help Java pros develop a resilient and portable application:

Character encoding
Different OSs can work with different character encodings. Understanding what they are and how to set them up can prevent your application from presenting weird characters.

TCP/IP networking
Cloud-native applications are distributed systems. In a world of cloud, internet, and network, understanding how to route tables, latency, fire-

walls, and everything related to TCP/IP networking is important, especially when things don't work as expected.

HTTP protocol
In a world where the browser is the client, understanding how HTTP 1.1 and 2.0 work can help you design your application better. Knowing what happens when you store your data in an HTTP session, especially in a multiclustered environment, can be quite helpful.

It's even good to know what frameworks are doing under the hood. Here we can take object relational mapping (ORM) frameworks like JPA and Hibernate as examples:

Enable SQL output during development
With SQL output enabled, you can see what commands are being sent to the database before finding out an odd SQL call is behaving badly.

Query fetch size
Most JPA/Hibernate implementations have a default fetch size of one (1). That means that if your query brings 1,000 entities from the database, 1,000 SQL commands will be executed to populate those entities. You can tune the fetch size to reduce the number of SQL instructions performed. You can identify this problem by having the SQL output enabled (see previous item).

One-to-many and many-to-one relationships
Although one-to-many relationships are lazy loaded by default, some developers make the mistake of changing the relationship to eager load the entities or manually initialize them before returning the collection of entities. Be careful about doing that because each eager-loaded entity can also create the *many-to-one* relationship, causing you to fetch almost every table/entity from the database. Enabling SQL output can help you to identify this problem as well (again, see first item).

In short, don't let yourself be controlled—be in control!

The Rebirth of Java

Sander Mak

Java has been declared dead perhaps more than any other programming language, it seems. Perhaps unsurprisingly, reports of its death are greatly exaggerated. Java has an enormous footprint in backend development, and most enterprises develop systems in Java. However, there's a kernel of truth in every rumor—Java was a slow-moving language in the age of dynamic languages like Ruby and JavaScript. Traditionally, major Java releases spanned three to four years of development. It's hard to keep up with other platforms at this pace.

In 2017, all this changed. Oracle—Java's steward—announced the Java platform would be released twice a year. Java 9, released toward the end of 2017, was the last big and long-awaited release. After Java 9, every year in March and September a new major Java release is delivered. Like clockwork.

Switching to this time-based release schedule has many consequences. Releases can no longer wait on features that are not yet complete. Also, because there's less time between releases and the team developing Java remains the same size, fewer features make it into a release. But that's OK—we get another release in only six months. A steady stream of new features and improvements is what we can count on.

Interestingly, new language features are now also delivered incrementally. The Java language is now evolving in a more agile manner. For example, Java 12 shipped Switch Expressions as a preview language feature, with the express intent of later extending this feature to support full pattern matching.

One of the reasons why Java releases took so much time and effort is that the platform became somewhat ossified in its 20-plus years of existence. In Java 9, the platform is fully modularized. Every part of the platform is now put into its own module, with explicit dependencies on other parts. The module system introduced in Java 9 ensures this platform architecture is adhered to from now on.

Platform internals are now safely encapsulated inside modules, preventing (ab)use by application and library code. Previously, many applications and libraries depended on these platform internals, making it hard to evolve Java without breaking lots of existing code. It's also possible to use the module system for your own applications. It can make your codebase more maintainable, flexible, and future-proof as well.

Moving from a long and unpredictable release cycle to regular calendar-based releases is a great achievement by the Java team. Adapting to this new reality has definitely taken time for us as a developer community. Fortunately, the changes in Java are now smaller and more incremental. These more frequent and regular releases are easier to adopt and adapt to.

For slower movers, a version of Java is marked as Long-Term Supported (LTS) every six releases, starting with Java 11. Meaning, you can move between LTS releases every three years if you want. It's important to understand that the LTS commitment is offered by vendors like Oracle, Red Hat, or even Amazon, and is not necessarily free of charge. In any case, the vendor-neutral OpenJDK project keeps producing supported builds for the latest Java release that is developed. Many things may and will change in releases between the LTS releases, though. If you can, hop on the frequent-release train and enjoy a steady stream of better Java. It's not as scary as it may sound.

Rediscover the JVM Through Clojure

James Elliott

Sometime around 2007, my office book club read *Java Concurrency in Practice* by Brian Goetz (Addison-Wesley). We weren't far past the preface of this important book when we panicked about how wrong our naive understanding of Java's memory model had been, and how easily bugs are introduced into multithreaded code. There were audible gasps, and at least one reported nightmare.

In developing a highly concurrent cloud offering, we needed a language that wouldn't litter our codebase with landmines of shared, mutable state. We chose Clojure: it has solid concurrency answers and favors functional, efficient transformation of immutable data. It runs on the familiar JVM, interoperating smoothly with the huge ecosystem of Java libraries. Though some were hesitant about the unfamiliar Lisp syntax and about relearning how to program without mutating variables, it was a great decision.

We discovered the benefits of a REPL-centric (read–eval–print loop) workflow:

- No rebuilding or relaunching to test changes
- Exploring the running system and trying variations instantly
- Building and refining ideas incrementally

We appreciated Clojure's bias toward working with data using standard structures and its rich, opinionated core library. You don't have to create lots of classes—each with its own mutually incompatible API—to model anything.

I rediscovered joy and energy in programming. A talk at the Strange Loop conference about live-coding musical performances in Clojure using Overtone (*https://oreil.ly/VcM79*) made me wonder: if Clojure was fast enough to make music, surely it could run stage lighting? That led to Afterglow (*https://*

oreil.ly/L9wjF), a project that consumed me for a while. Figuring out how to write lighting effects in a functional style was a puzzle, but Overtone's functional metronome inspired my effect functions, mapping musical time to lighting positions, colors, and intensities.

I relearned trigonometry and linear algebra to aim different lights at the same point in space. I discovered how to create a desired color using a fixture's different-hued LEDs. Live-coding stage lighting is a ton of fun.

Then I wanted to synchronize Afterglow's metronome with tracks playing on the CDJs (*https://oreil.ly/utaDV*) (today's digital DJ turntables) I use to mix music. Their protocol is proprietary and undocumented, but I was determined. I set up a network sniffer and figured it out (*https://oreil.ly/FIIIk*). Early success led to excited contributions from around the world, so I wrote the library Beat Link (*https://oreil.ly/fhvT2*) to make using what we learned easy. I wrote it in Java to be widely understandable but discovered that using Clojure had made writing Java feel cumbersome.

People built on it and ported it to other languages. I created a quick demo for a show producer on using Beat Link to trigger MIDI events that his video software and lighting console could respond to. It became my most popular project because it's useful to nonprogrammers. Artists are still doing cool new things with Beat Link Trigger (*https://oreil.ly/JEK1H*) all the time, and as a guest at music festivals and touring shows, I've seen the results. Since it's Clojure, users can extend it, and their code gets byte-compiled and loaded into the JVM as if it were part of the project all along—another secret weapon Clojure can give you.

I encourage anyone working in Java to take a serious look at Clojure, and see how it can change your experience of life on the JVM.

Refactor Boolean Values to Enumerations

Peter Hilton

You wouldn't use "magic numbers" in your code, so don't use magic Booleans either! Boolean literals are worse than hardcoded numbers: a 42 in the code might look familiar, but false could be anything, and anything could be false.

When two variables are both true, you don't know whether that's a coincidence or whether they're both "true" for the same reason and should change together. This makes the code harder to read, and causes bugs when you read it wrong. As with magic numbers, you should refactor to named constants.

Refactoring 42 to an ASCII_ASTERISK or EVERYTHING constant improves code readability, and so does refactoring true to a Boolean constant called AVAILABLE in a Product class, for example. However, you probably shouldn't have any Boolean fields in your domain model: some Boolean values aren't really Boolean.

Suppose your Product entity has a Boolean available field, to indicate whether the product is currently being sold. This isn't really a Boolean: it's an optional "available" value, which isn't the same thing because "not available" really means something else, like "out of stock."

When a type has two possible values, that's a coincidence, and can change—by adding a "discontinued" option, for example. The existing Boolean field cannot accommodate the additional value.

Beware: using null to mean something is the worst possible way to implement a third value. You'll end up needing a code comment like "true when the product is available, false when out of stock, null when discontinued." Please don't do that.

The most obvious model for products you no longer sell is a Boolean discontinued field, in addition to the available field. This works, but is harder to maintain because there's no hint that these fields are related. Fortunately, Java has a way to group named constants.

Refactor related Boolean fields like these to a Java *enum type*:

```java
enum ProductAvailability {
    AVAILABLE, OUT_OF_STOCK, DISCONTINUED, BANNED
}
```

Enum types are great because then you get more things to name. Also, the values are more readable than a `true` that means that the value is really some other value, such as `AVAILABLE`. Enum types also turn out to be more convenient than you might expect, which makes laziness a weak excuse for not refactoring.

The enum type can still have Boolean convenience methods, which you might want if your original code had lots of conditional checks for available products. In fact, enum types go further than simply grouping constants, with fields, constructors, and methods. A less obvious but more important benefit is that you now have a destination for other refactorings that move availability-related logic to the `ProductAvailability` type.

Serializing an enum type is more work, e.g., than using JSON or a database. However, it's less than you might expect. You're probably already using a library that handles this nicely and lets you choose how to serialize to a Single Value Object representation.

Domain models often suffer from *primitive obsession*—overuse of Java primitive types. Refactoring numbers and dates to domain classes allows your code to become more expressive and readable, and the new types provide a better home for related code, such as validations and comparisons.

In the problem domain's language, Boolean types are false, and enumerated types are the truth.

Refactoring Toward Speed-Reading

Benjamin Muskalla

A casual reader usually reaches 150–200 wpm (words per minute) with a good comprehension rate. People who are into speed-reading can easily reach up to 700 wpm. But don't worry, we don't need to set a new world record for speed-reading to learn the basic concepts and apply them to our code. We'll look at three areas that are particularly helpful when it comes to reading code: skimming, meta guiding, and visual fixation.

So what makes speed-reading that fast? One of the first steps is to suppress subvocalization. Subvocalization? Exactly. That voice in your head that just tried to properly articulate that word. And yes, you're now aware of that voice. But don't worry, it will go away soon! Subvocalization can be unlearned and is an essential first step to seriously improve reading speed.

Let's look at this method with three parameters, which all need validating. One way to read the code is to follow where and how the input parameters are used:

```
public void printReport(Header header, Body body, Footer footer) {
  checkNotNull(header, "header must not be null");
  validate(body);
  checkNotNull(footer, "footer must not be null");
}
```

After locating `header`, we have to find the next parameter, `body`, which requires us to look down and left. We can start with a simple refactoring to align the first and third check so we only break the horizontal flow once:

```
public void printReport(Header header, Body body, Footer footer) {
  checkNotNull(header, "header must not be null");
  checkNotNull(footer, "footer must not be null");
  validate(body);
}
```

Alternatively, given that checking for null is a validation of the parameter as well, we could extract the checkNotNull method calls into their own properly named methods to help guide the reader. Whether these are the same or overloaded version of the method depends on the code at hand:

```
public void printReport(Header header, Body body, Footer footer) {
    validateReportElement(header);
    validateReportElement(body);
    validateReportElement(footer);
}
```

Meta guiding is another technique for speed-reading. Instead of trying to read word by word in a book, you try to capture the whole line at once. Children usually do that by using their finger to keep track of the word they're reading. Using some sort of guidance helps us to keep moving forward and avoid jumping back a word or two. Funny enough, code itself can act as such a device as it has an inherent structure that we can leverage to guide our eye:

```
List<String> items = new ArrayList<>(zeros);
items.add("one");
items.add("two");
items.add("three");
```

How many items are in the list? One, two, three! Actually, it's four. Maybe more. Oops, missed that zeros argument too? The structure that should help us actually gets in our way. While we have allowed our reader to be guided by the alignment of the add methods, we totally misguided the eye and missed the constructor argument. Rewriting this allows the reader to follow the guide easily without missing any important information:

```
List<String> items = new ArrayList<>();
items.addAll(zeros);
items.add("one");
items.add("two");
items.add("three");
```

Next time you write a piece of code, see if you can speed-read it. Keep in mind the basics about visual fixation and meta guiding. Try to find a structure that makes logical sense while guiding the eye to see the relevant information. Not only will it help you to read code faster in the future but it also helps keep you in the flow.

Simple Value Objects

Steve Freeman

Classes that represent Value Objects don't need getters or setters. Java developers are usually taught to use getters for accessing fields, like this:

```
public class Coordinate {
    private Latitude latitude;
    private Longitude longitude;

    public Coordinate(Latitude latitude, Longitude longitude) {
        this.latitude = latitude;
        this.longitude = longitude;
    }

    /**
     * @return the latitude of the Coordinate
     */
    public Latitude getLatitude() {
        return latitude;
    }

     /**
      * @return the longitude of the Coordinate
      */
    public Longitude getLongitude() {
        return longitude;
    }
}
```

```
System.out.println(thing.getLatitude());
```

The idea is that getters encapsulate how values are represented in an object, providing a consistent approach across a codebase. It also allows for protection against *aliasing*, for example, by cloning collections before returning them.

The style has its origins in the early days of JavaBeans, when there was a lot of interest in graphical tooling using reflection. There might also have been some influence from Smalltalk (the classic object-oriented language), in which all fields are private unless exposed *via* an accessor; read-only fields have getters, but no setters.

In practice, not all classes play the same role and, lacking an alternative structure in the language, many coders write Java classes that are actually *Value Objects*: a simple set of fields that never change, where equality is based on value rather than identity. In our example, two `Coordinate` objects that have the same latitude and longitude are effectively the same. I can use instances of `Coordinate` as constants throughout my code because they're immutable.

Some years ago, I, like many of my colleagues, started to tire of the boilerplate duplication that getters require and simplified my style for Value Objects. I made all the fields `public final`, like a C `struct`:

```java
public class Coordinate {
    public final Latitude latitude;
    public final Longitude longitude;

    public Coordinate(Latitude latitude, Longitude longitude) {
        this.latitude = latitude;
        this.longitude = longitude;
    }
}


    System.out.println(coordinate.latitude);
```

I can do this because the object is immutable (again, one has to be careful about aliasing if any of the values are structured), and I tend to avoid inheritance or implementing much behavior. This represents a change in approach from the earlier days of Java. For example, `java.awt.Point` is mutable, and the move method updates its x and y fields in place. Nowadays, after twenty years of improvements in the JVM and wider adoption of functional programming, such transient objects are cheap enough that we would expect move to return a new immutable copy with the new location. An example for our `Coordinate` would be:

```
public class Coordinate {
    public Coordinate atLatitude(Latitude latitude) {
        return new Coordinate(latitude, this.longitude);
    }
}
```

I've found simplified Value Objects to be a useful convention for clarifying the role of a type, with less distracting noise in the code. They're easy to refactor into and often provide a useful target for accumulating methods that express the domain of the code better. Occasionally, the behavioral features of a Value Object become more significant, and I find I can express what I need with methods and make the fields private.

It also turns out that the Java language team has recognized this too and introduced a record structure in Java 14. Until this is widespread, we'll have to rely on convention.

Take Care of Your Module Declarations

Nicolai Parlog

If you're creating Java modules, your module declarations (*module-info.java* files) are easily your most important source files. Each one represents an entire JAR and governs how it interacts with other JARs, so take good care of your declarations! Here are a few things to look out for.

Keep Module Declarations Clean

Module declarations are code and should be treated as such, so make sure your code style is applied. Beyond that, rather than placing directives randomly, structure your module declarations. Here's the order the JDK uses:

1. Requires, including static and transitive

2. Exports

3. Exports to

4. Opens

5. Opens to

6. Uses

7. Provides

Whatever you decide, if you have a document defining your code style, record the decision there. If you have your IDE, build tool, or code analyzer check such things for you, even better. Try to bring it up to speed so it can automatically check—or even apply—your chosen style.

Comment Module Declarations

Opinions on code documentation, like Javadoc or inline comments, vary wildly, but whatever your team's position on comments is, extend it to module declarations. If you like abstractions to have a sentence or two explaining their meaning and importance, add such a Javadoc comment to each module. Even if that's not your style, most people agree that it's good to document *why* a specific decision was made. In a module declaration, that could mean adding an inline comment to:

- An optional dependency to explain why the module might be absent
- A qualified export to explain why it isn't public API, but is partially accessible
- An open package explaining which frameworks are expected to access it

Module declarations present a new opportunity: never before has it been this easy to document the relationships of your project's artifacts in code.

Review Module Declarations

Module declarations are the central representation of your modular structure, and examining them should be an integral part of any kind of code review you do. Whether it's looking over your changes before a commit or before opening a pull request, wrapping up after a pair-programming session, or during a formal code review, anytime you inspect a body of code, pay special attention to *module-info.java*:

- Are new module dependencies necessary (consider replacement with services) and in line with the project's architecture?
- Is the code prepared to handle the absence of optional dependencies?
- Are new package exports necessary? Are all public classes in there ready for use? Can you reduce the API surface area?
- Does it make sense that an export is qualified, or is it a cop-out to get access to an API that's not ready to be public?
- Were changes made that could cause problems for downstream consumers that are not part of the build process?

Investing time into diligently reviewing module descriptors might sound like waste, but I see it as an opportunity: *never before has it been this easy to analyze and review the relationships of your project's artifacts and its structure.* And not the photographed whiteboard sketch that was uploaded to your wiki a few years ago; no, the real deal, the *actual* relationships between your artifacts. Module declarations show the naked reality instead of outdated good intentions.

Take Good Care of Your Dependencies

Brian Vermeer

Modern Java development is heavily dependent on third-party libraries. By using Maven or Gradle, we have easy mechanisms in place to import and use published packages. As developers do not want to create and maintain boilerplate functionality but rather focus on the specific business logic, using frameworks and libraries can be a wise choice.

When looking at an average project, the amount of your code can be as little as 1%, and the rest will be imported libraries and frameworks. A lot of code that is put into production is simply not ours, but we do depend on it heavily.

As we look at our code and the way we treat contributions by team members, we often turn to processes like code reviews before we merge new code into our master branch as a first-pass quality assurance measure. Alternatively, this quality control process might also be covered by practicing pair pro-gramming. The way we treat our dependencies, however, is very different from how we treat our own code. Dependencies are often just used without any form of validation. Importantly, the top-level dependencies, on many occasions, in turn pull in transitive dependencies that can go many levels deep. For example, a 200-line Spring application with 5 direct dependencies can end up using 60 dependencies in total, which amounts to almost half a million lines of code being shipped to production.

By only using these dependencies we blindly trust other people's code, which is odd compared to how we handle our own code.

Vulnerable Dependencies

From a security point of view, you should scan your dependencies for known vulnerabilities. If a vulnerability in a dependency is found and disclosed, you should be aware of this and replace or update those dependencies. Using out-dated dependencies with known vulnerabilities can be disastrous if you look at some examples in the past.

By scanning your dependencies during every step in your development process, you might prevent that vulnerable dependency surprise before you ship your code to production.

You should also keep scanning your production snapshot, as new vulnerabilities may be disclosed while you are already using it in your production environment.

Updating Dependencies

You should choose your dependencies wisely. Look at how well a library or framework is maintained and how many contributors are working on it. Depending on outdated or poorly maintained libraries is a large risk. If you want to stay up-to-date, you can use your package manager to help you detect if newer versions are available. By using the Maven or Gradle version plug-in, you can use the following commands to check for newer versions:

- Maven: `mvn versions:display-dependency-updates`
- Gradle: `gradle dependencyUpdates -Drevision=release`

A Strategy for Your Dependencies

When handling dependencies in your system, you should have a strategy in place. Questions about dependency health and the reason why a particular dependency is used should be made explicit. Next, you should also carefully think about what your update strategy should be. Updating often is considered less painful in general. Last, but not least, you should have tooling in place that scans your libraries for known vulnerabilities to prevent being breached.

In any case, you should take good care of your dependencies and choose the right library with the right version for the right reason.

Take "Separation of Concerns" Seriously

Dave Farley

If you studied computer science, you may have learned about an idea called *separation of concerns.*[1] This is best characterized by the sound byte "One class one thing, one method one thing." The idea is that your classes and methods (and functions) should always be focused on a single outcome.

Think carefully about the responsibilities of your classes and methods. I sometimes teach classes in test-driven design. I use adding fractions as a simple coding kata to explore TDD. The most common first test I see people write often looks something like this:

```
assertEquals("2/3", Fractions.addFraction("1/3", "1/3"));
```

For me, this test is screaming "poor design." First, where is the fraction? It only exists implicitly, presumably inside the addFraction function.

Worse than this, let's think about what is going on here. How would we describe the behavior of the addFraction function? Perhaps something like "It takes two strings, parses them, and calculates their sum." As soon as you see, or think, the word "and" in the description of a function, method, or class, you should hear alarm bells ringing inside your head. There are two concerns here: one is string parsing, and the other is fraction adding.

What if we wrote our test like this instead:

```
Fraction fraction = new Fraction(1, 3);
assertEquals(new Fraction(2,3), fraction.add(new Fraction(1, 3)));
```

How would we describe the add method in this second example? Perhaps, "It returns the sum of the two fractions." This second solution is simpler to

---

1 "Separation of concerns" was first mentioned by Edsger W. Dijkstra (*https://oreil.ly/Hyfse*) in his 1974 paper "On the Role of Scientific Thought," which was published in *Selected Writings on Computing: A Personal Perspective* (New York: Springer-Verlag, 1982), 60–66.

implement, simpler to test, and the code inside will be simpler to understand. It is also significantly more flexible because it is more modular and therefore more composable. For example, if we wanted to add three fractions instead of two, how would that work? In the first example, we would have to add a second method or refactor the first, so we could call something like:

```
assertEquals("5/6", Fractions.addFraction("1/3", "1/3", "1/6"));
```

In the second case, no code changes are necessary:

```
Fraction fraction1 = new Fraction(1, 3);
Fraction fraction2 = new Fraction(1, 3);
Fraction fraction3 = new Fraction(1, 6);

assertEquals(new Fraction(5,6),
             fraction1.add(fraction2).add(fraction3));
```

Let's imagine that we did want to start with a string representation. We could add a new, second class called something like `FractionParser` or `StringTo Fraction`:

```
assertEquals(new Fraction(1, 3),
             StringFractionTranslator.createFraction("1/3"));
```

`StringFractionTranslator.createFraction` converts a string representation of a fraction into a `Fraction`. We could imagine other methods on this class that take a `Fraction` and render a `String`. Now we can test this code more thoroughly, and we can test it separately from the complexity of adding fractions, or multiplying them or anything else.

Test-driven development is very helpful in this respect because it highlights issues of poor separation of concerns clearly. It is often the case that if you are finding it difficult to write a test, it is a result of either poor coupling in your design or poor separation of concerns.

Separating concerns is a very effective design strategy to employ in any code. Code with good separation of concerns is, by definition, more modular, and it's usually much more composable, flexible, testable, and readable too.

Always strive to make every single method, class, and function focused on a single outcome. As soon as you notice that your code is trying to do two things, pull out a new class or method to make it simpler and clearer.

Technical Interviewing Is a Skill Worth Developing

Trisha Gee

I'm going to let you into a secret: our industry is *horrible* at interviewing developers. What's really silly is that we almost never sit a candidate down to write actual code in the actual environment they're going to be developing in. That's like testing a musician on theory but never listening to them play.

The good news is that interviewing is a skill like any other, meaning it can be learned. As with acquiring any other skill, you can research what's involved and practice, practice, practice. If you get rejected during interviews, it doesn't mean you're not a good developer. It might just mean you're not good at interviews. That's something you can improve on, and each interview is another opportunity to gather more data and to practice.

Interviewers will often ask similar sorts of questions. Here are three that are fairly typical:

Multithreading gotchas

It's still common to be asked to inspect code with `synchronized` scattered liberally around and find the race condition or deadlock. Organizations with this sort of code have bigger problems than hiring developers (although if they show that code in interviews, they'll definitely have a problem hiring developers), so maybe you don't want to work there anyway. Having a working understanding of concurrency in Java (*https://oreil.ly/n54xA*) will help you navigate most of these interview questions. If you don't know old-school Java concurrency, talk about how modern Java has abstracted away these problems and explain how you might use Fork/Join (*https://oreil.ly/CEQjL*) or parallel streams (*https://oreil.ly/epUKa*) instead.

Compiler gotchas

"Does this code compile?" Well, I dunno, that's what a computer and IDE are for—the tools can answer the question while I worry about other things. If you get asked these sorts of questions in interviews, use some of the Java Certification study materials (for example, actual books) to learn how to answer them.

Data structures

Java data structures are fairly straightforward: understanding the difference between a `List` (*https://oreil.ly/tc6p4*), a `Set` (*https://oreil.ly/KP1BA*), and a `Map` (*https://oreil.ly/37mGa*) is a good place to start. Knowing what a hash code (*https://oreil.ly/DvSYa*) is for helps, and so does how `equals` (*https://oreil.ly/QvlLo*) is used in the contexts of collections.

A quick web search for *common java interview questions* will also give you a good set of topics to research.

Is this cheating? If you learn just enough to get through the interview, will you really know enough to do the job? Remember: our industry is horrible at interviewing developers. The interview experience is often miles away from the job experience. Ask plenty of questions to see if you can get a glimpse of what working there is really like. You can learn new technologies easily enough—that's what we do all the time. It's all that *people-related* stuff that often determines whether you'll succeed. But that's a topic for another article.

Test-Driven Development

Dave Farley

Test-driven development (TDD) is widely misunderstood. Before TDD, the only thing that applied pressure for high quality in software was the knowledge, experience, and commitment of a programmer. After TDD, there was something else.

High quality in software is widely agreed to include the following properties in code:

- Modularity
- Loose coupling
- Cohesion
- Good separation of concerns
- Information hiding

Testable code has those properties. TDD is development (design) driven by tests. In TDD, we write the test before writing code that makes the test pass. TDD is much more than "good unit testing."

Writing the test first is important; it means that we always end up with "testable" code. It also means that coverage is never an issue. If we write the test first, we always have great coverage and don't need to worry about it as a metric—and it is a poor metric.

TDD amplifies the talent of a software developer. It doesn't make bad programmers great, but it makes any programmer better.

TDD is very simple—the process is *Red, Green, Refactor*:

- We write a test and see it fail (Red).
- We write the minimum code to make it pass and see it pass (Green).
- We refactor the code, and the test, to make them as clean, expressive, elegant, and simple as we can (Refactor).

These steps represent three distinct phases in the design of our code. We should be thinking differently during each of these steps.

Red

Focus on expressing the behavioral intent of your code. Concentrate only on the public interface of your code. That is all that we are designing at this point—nothing else.

Think only about how to write a nice, clear test that captures just what you would like your code to do.

Focus on the design of the public interface by making the test simple to write. If your ideas are easy to express in your test, they will also be easy to express when someone uses your code.

Green

Do the simplest thing that makes the test pass. Even if that simple thing seems naive. As long as the test is failing, your code is broken, and you are at an unstable point in the development. Get back to safety (Green) as quickly and simply as you can.

Your tests should grow to form a "behavioral specification" for your code. Adopting the discipline of writing code only when you have a failing test helps to better elaborate and evolve that specification.

Refactor

Once back to *Green*, you can safely refactor. This keeps you honest and stops you from wandering off into the weeds and getting lost! Make small simple steps, and then rerun the tests to confirm that everything still works.

Refactoring is not an afterthought. This is an opportunity to think more strategically about your design. If the setup of your tests is too complex, your code probably has poor separation of concerns and may be too tightly coupled to other things. If you need to include too many other classes to test your code, perhaps your code is not very cohesive.

Practice a pause for refactoring every time you achieve a passing test. Always look and reflect, "Could I do this better?" The three phases of TDD are distinct, and your mental focus should also be distinct to maximize the benefit of each phase.

There Are Great Tools in Your bin/ Directory

Rod Hilton

Every Java developer is familiar with `javac` for compiling, `java` for running, and probably `jar` for packaging Java applications. However, many other useful tools come installed with the JDK. They are already on your computer in your JDK's *bin/* directory and are invokable from your PATH. It's good to get acquainted with some of these tools so you know what's at your disposal:

jps

> If you've ever found yourself running `ps aux | grep java` to find the running JVMs, you probably just want to run `jps`. This dedicated tool lists all the running JVMs, but instead of showing you a lengthy command with `CLASSPATHs` and arguments, `jps` simply lists the process ID and the application's main class name, making it far easier to figure out which process is which. `jps -l` will list the fully qualified main class name, `jps -m` will show the arguments passed to the main method, and `jps -v` will show all the arguments passed to the JVM itself.

javap

> The JDK comes with a Java class file disassembler. Run `javap <class file>` to see that class file's fields and methods, which can often be very enlightening for understanding what code written in JVM-based languages such as Scala, Clojure, or Groovy is turned into under the hood. Run `javap -c <class file>` to see the complete bytecode of those methods.

jmap

> Running `jmap -heap <process id>` will print a summary of the JVM process's memory space, such as how much memory is being used in each of the JVM's memory generations, as well as the heap configuration and type of GC being used. `jmap -histo <process id>` will print a histogram of each class in the heap, how many instances there are of that

class, and how many bytes of memory are consumed. Most critically, running `jmap -dump:format=b,file=<filename> <process id>` will dump a snapshot of the entire heap to a file.

jhat

Running `jhat <heap dump file>` will take the file generated by `jmap` and run a local web server. You can connect to this server in a browser to explore the heap space interactively, grouped by package name. The "Show instance counts for all classes (excluding platform)" link shows only instances of classes outside of Java itself. You can also run "OQL" queries, allowing you to query the heap space via SQL-esque syntax.

jinfo

Run `jinfo <process id>` to see all system properties the JVM loaded with and JVM command-line flags.

jstack

Running `jstack <process id>` will print stack traces for all current Java threads running in a JVM.

jconsole *and* jvisualvm

These are graphical tools that allow connecting to JVMs and interactively monitoring running JVMs. They offer visual graphs and histograms of various aspects of a running process and are a mouse-friendly alternative to many of the tools listed above.

jshell

As of Java 9, Java has an honest-to-goodness REPL—a great tool to check syntax, run quick Java-based commands, or try out code and experiment without building full programs.

Many of these tools can run not only locally but against JVM processes running on remote machines as well. These are only some of the useful programs you already have installed; take some time to see what else is in your JDK's directory of executables and read their man pages—it's always handy to know what tools are in your toolbelt.

Think Outside the Java Sandbox

Ian F. Darwin

"Java is the best language ever, for every purpose." If you believe this, you need to get out more. Sure, Java's a great language, but it's not the only good language, nor the best for every purpose. In fact, every so often you should—as a professional developer—take the time to learn and use a new language, either at work or on your own. Go deep enough to recognize how it differs in some fundamental way from what you're used to and whether it might be useful in your projects. In other words: try it, you might like it. Here are a few languages you may want to learn:

- JavaScript is the language of the browser. Despite similar names and a dozen or so keywords, JavaScript and Java are very different. JavaScript comes with hundreds of different web frameworks, some of which go beyond the frontend. For example, Node.js (*https://nodejs.org*) lets you run JavaScript server-side, which opens up many new possibilities.

- Kotlin (*https://kotlinlang.org*) is a JVM language that, like most of these languages, has a more relaxed syntax than Java, along with other features that can give it an advantage over Java. Google uses Kotlin for much of its work in Android and encourages its use in Android apps. 'Nuff said!

- Dart (*https://dartlang.org*) and Flutter (*https://flutter.dev*): Dart is a compiled scripting language from Google. Originally for web programming, it didn't blossom until Flutter began using Dart for Android and iOS apps (and browser-side, someday) from one codebase.

- Python (*https://www.python.org*), Ruby (*https://oreil.ly/jtdUQ*), and Perl (*https://www.perl.org*) have been around for decades and remain among the most popular languages. The first two have JVM implementations, Jython and JRuby, though the former isn't being actively maintained.

- Scala (*https://oreil.ly/iJX8Q*), Clojure (*http://clojure.org*), and Frege (*https://oreil.ly/vXlmZ*) (an implementation of Haskell (*https://*

www.haskell.org)) are JVM functional programming (*https://oreil.ly/ u0BQX*) (FP) languages. FP has a long, narrow history, but has been making inroads into the mainstream in recent years. Many FP languages don't run on the JVM as of this writing, such as Idris (*https://oreil.ly/ YS0vJ*) and Agda (*https://oreil.ly/X8wti*). Learning FP may help you to use the functional facilities in Java 8+, if you're not really comfortable there.

- R (*https://oreil.ly/eh0Tw*) is an interpreted language for data manipulation. Cloned (*https://oreil.ly/PbWQW*) from Bell Labs' S (*https://oreil.ly/ yDxJZ*) for statisticians, R is now popular with data scientists or anyone going "beyond the spreadsheet." Lots of stats, math, and graphics functions built-ins and add-ons.

- Rust (*https://oreil.ly/Shxzu*) is a compiled language aimed at systems development with features for concurrency and strong typing.

- Go (*https://golang.org*) ("Golang") is a compiled language invented at Google by Robert Griesemer, Rob Pike, and Ken Thompson (cocreator of Unix). There are multiple compilers, targeting different operating systems natively and web development by compiling down to JavaScript and WebAssembly.

- C is ancestral to C++, Objective-C, and, to some extent, Java, C#, and Rust. (C gave these languages the basic syntax of built-in types, method syntax, and curly braces for code blocks and is the language to blame for `int i = 077;` having the value 63 in Java.) If you didn't learn assembly language, "C level" is a place to start understanding memory models that will give you an appreciation for Java's way of doing things.

- JShell (*https://oreil.ly/vkgl3*) isn't a language, per se—it's a different way of doing Java. Instead of having to write out `public class Mumble { and public static void main(String[] args) {` just to try out an expression or some new API, just forget all the ceremony and boilerplate and use JShell.

So go on. Step outside of Java.

Thinking in Coroutines

*Dawn Griffiths and
David Griffiths*

Coroutines are functions or methods that can be suspended and resumed. In Kotlin, they can be used in place of threads for asynchronous work because many coroutines can run efficiently on a single thread.

To see how coroutines work, we're going to create an example program that plays these drum sequences in parallel:

Instrument	Sequence
Toms	x-x-x-x-x-x-x-x-
High hat	x-x-x---x-x-x---
Crash cymbal	---------------x----

We *could* use threads to do this, but in most systems, the sound is played by the sound subsystem, while the code pauses until it can play the next sound. It's wasteful to block a valuable resource like a thread in this way.

Instead, we're going to create a set of coroutines: one for each of the instruments. We'll have a method called `playBeats`, which takes a drum sequence and the name of a sound file. The full code is at *https://oreil.ly/6x0GK*; a simplified version looks like this:

```
suspend fun playBeats(beats: String, file: String) {
  for (...) { // for each beat
    ...
    playSound(file)
    ...
    delay(<time in milliseconds>)
    ...
  }
}
```

Call this with playBeats("x-x-x---x-x-x---", "high_hat.aiff"), and it will play the sequence using the *high_hat.aiff* sound file. There are two things in this code that you find in any Kotlin coroutine:

- It begins with the suspend keyword, which means that the function can suspend its operation at some point until some external code restarts it.
- It includes a nonblocking call to the delay function.

The delay function is analogous to something like Thread.sleep, except it works by handing back control to the outside world, with a request to resume again after the specified pause.

If that's what a coroutine looks like, how do you call it? What calls the coroutine, copes with it suspending, and then reschedules it when it needs to restart? The launch function takes care of everything for us. The main method to run the coroutines looks like this:

```kotlin
fun main() {
  runBlocking {
    launch { playBeats("x-x-x-x-x-x-x-", "toms.aiff") }
    launch { playBeats("x-x-x---x-x-x---", "high_hat.aiff") }
    launch { playBeats("----------------x----", "crash_cymbal.aiff") }
  }
}
```

Each call to launch accepts a block of code that calls the coroutine. A block of code in Kotlin is like a lambda in Java. The launch function registers the coroutine call with a scope provided by the runBlocking function.

runBlocking runs a scheduling loop on the main thread, which coordinates the calls to each of the coroutines. It calls each of the playBeats coroutines in turn and waits for it to suspend by calling delay. runBlocking then waits until some other playBeats coroutine needs to resume. runBlocking does this until all the coroutines complete.

You can think of coroutines as lightweight threads: they allow you to mentally split work into separate simple tasks, which appear to run concurrently while running on the same thread.

Coroutines are invaluable when writing code for Android, which enforces a strict threading model in which some operations must run on the main UI thread. But they're also useful for creating scalable server-side applications that must make efficient use of existing threads.

Threads Are Infrastructure; Treat Them as Such

Russel Winder

How many Java programmers manage—or even think about—stack use during their programming? More or less none. The vast majority of Java programmers leave stack management to the compiler and runtime system.

How many Java programmers manage—or even think about—heap use during their programming? Very few. The majority of Java programmers assume the garbage collection system will deal with all heap management.

So why are so many Java programmers managing all their threads manually? Because that is what they were taught to do. From the beginning, Java supported shared memory multithreading, which was almost certainly a big error.

Almost all that most Java programmers know about concurrency and parallelism is founded on the theory of constructing operating systems from the 1960s. If you are writing an operating system then this is all good stuff, but are most Java programs actually operating systems? No. So a rethink is in order.

If your code has any synchronized statements, locks, mutexes—all the paraphernalia of operating systems—then in all likelihood, you are doing it wrong. This is the wrong level of abstraction for most Java programmers. Just as stack space and heap space are managed resources, threads should be considered managed resources. Instead of creating threads explicitly and managing them, construct tasks and submit them to a thread pool. Tasks should be single threaded—obviously! If you have many tasks that need to communicate with one another, then rather than using shared memory, use a thread-safe queue instead.

All of this was already known in the 1970s, culminating in Sir Charles Antony (Tony) Richard Hoare creating Communicating Sequential Processes (CSP) as an algebra for describing concurrent and parallel computation. Sadly, it was ignored by the majority of programmers in the rush to use shared memory multithreading, with every program being a new operating system. During the 2000s, though, many looked to get back to sequential processes communicating. Perhaps the most high profile advocate of this in recent years has been the Go programming language. It is all about sequential processes communicating, made to execute via an underlying thread pool.

Many use the terms actors, dataflow, CSP, or active objects, all of which are variations on the sequential process and communication theme. Akka, Quasar, and GPars are all frameworks providing various forms of task over a thread pool. The Java platform comes with the Fork/Join framework, which can be used explicitly and also underpins the Streams library, the revolution of Java introduced in Java 8.

Threads as a managed resource is the correct level of abstraction for the vast majority of Java programmers. Actors, dataflow, CSP, and active objects are the abstractions for the vast majority of programmers to use. Giving up manual control over threads releases Java programmers to write simpler, more comprehensible, more maintainable systems.

The Three Traits of Really, Really Good Developers

Jannah Patchay

My undergraduate degree was in computer science and math, and the first few years of my career were spent working as a Java developer. I really enjoyed my time as a developer. Like many mathematicians, I had an obsession with writing clean and elegant code, and I would refactor my code for ages until it was as near to perfection as it could get. I was aware of the end users, but only to the extent that they provided the requirements that created the challenges that I would then have to solve.

Fast-forward to 20 years after I graduated, and I'm now on a completely different path, consulting on financial markets regulation and market structure, with a particular interest in financial innovation, which also keeps me in touch with my techie roots. I've worked with many developers over the years, from the other side of the fence as the person who provides and clarifies the requirements. And over time, I've developed a greater appreciation of certain traits that really, really good developers have that go beyond technical ability.

The first and most important is curiosity. The same drive that causes you to want to solve problems, to understand how things work, and to build new things, can and should be applied to your interactions with your clients and stakeholders. It's great when developers ask lots of questions about the business domain because it shows that they really want to understand and to learn. It also leads to a better understanding of the business domain and the ability to address the problems of end users more effectively. I've encountered loads of development managers who actively dissuade their teams from "bothering" the business too much with questions. That's so wrong.

The second and third are empathy and imagination. It's about the ability to put yourself in your end user's shoes and try to understand their priorities and experience of using your software. It's also the ability to then come up with creative solutions to the challenges that they face, using your technical expertise. Many developers tend to dismiss a lot of this stuff as unimportant or to assume that it's for someone else to deal with. But it's much more effective, and makes you a better developer, if you are able to communicate directly with the business yourself.

These might sound like obvious things. But they are so important. I recently attended a conference on tech and innovation that focused on the importance of collaboration between technology and the business in order to best leverage emerging technologies like the cloud, distributed ledger technology, and artificial intelligence/machine learning. Many speakers emphasized the importance of breaking down walls between developers and end users. Some now embed developers into their business teams and expect them to know just as much about the business domain. So this is also about the future and about how to work smarter. If you can cultivate these skills, it can also open doors for you.

Trade-Offs in a Microservices Architecture

Kenny Bastani

Is there an optimal software architecture? What does it look like? How do we measure "optimal" when it comes to building and operating software? An optimal software architecture is one that has maximal flexibility for change at the lowest possible cost. Here, cost is measured in terms of certain qualities that represent a software architecture's design and implementation—in addition to the cost of the infrastructure to operate it. The defining trait of a software quality is that it can be tangibly measured and has an impact on other qualities.

For example, if a software architecture requires strong consistency guarantees, there is an impact on qualities like performance and availability. Eric Brewer created the CAP theorem to describe a set of measurable trade-offs where you can only choose two out of three guarantees for running a database: *consistency*, *availability*, and *partition tolerance*. The theorem states that when applications share state across the boundaries of a network, you must choose between consistency or availability, but you cannot have both.

One of the main problems with microservices is that there is no single comprehensive definition. Moreover, microservices are a collection of concepts and ideas that are based on a set of constraints for delivering a services architecture. A microservice, or any piece of software you build, is a history of choices—which will affect your ability to make new choices today.

Microservices may not have a single definition, but they do most commonly have the following characteristics:

- Independent deployability
- Organized around business capabilities
- Database per service

- One application, one team
- API-first
- Continuous delivery

As you go out into the world of software development, you will eventually find that there is no such thing as the right choice. Indeed, most developers or operators might believe there is a best choice, and you may find that they argue strongly in favor of that choice. As you encounter more and more opportunities to make a decision between multiple choices, for instance, which database to use, you'll eventually come to discover that all available options introduce certain trade-offs. That is, you will usually have to lose something to gain something.

Here is a short list of trade-offs you might encounter when making a decision to include a dependency for your microservice:

Availability	How often is my system available to its users?
Performance	What is the overall performance of my system?
Consistency	What guarantees does my system provide about consistency?
Speed	How fast can I deploy a single line of code change to production?
Composability	What percentage of an architecture and codebase can be reused instead of duplicated?
Compute	What is the cost of my system's compute under peak load?
Scalability	What is the cost of adding capacity if peak load continues to increase?
Marginality	What is the average diminishing marginal return of adding developers to my team?
Partition tolerance	If a partition in the network causes an outage or latency, will my application experience or cause a cascading failure?

How does answering one question affect answering the others?

You will find each of these questions often has some kind of relation to the other questions. If you ever find yourself making a tough decision in a software architecture that uses microservices, come back to this list of questions.

Uncheck Your Exceptions

Kevlin Henney

If you ever want to walk to hell, the journey will be easy on your feet. The whole road is very well paved, with good intentions as far as the eye can see. At least one of those paving stones is dedicated to Java's checked exception model.

A checked exception is one that, if not handled within a method, must appear in the method's `throws` clause. Any class descended from `Throwable` can be listed after `throws`, but unhandled checked exceptions (not descended from either `RuntimeException` or `Error`) *must* appear. This is a feature of the Java language, but it has no meaning for the JVM and is not a requirement for JVM languages.

The good intention here promotes a method's failures to the same type-level significance as its success-scenario inputs and outputs. At first sight, this seems reasonable. Indeed, in a small and closed codebase, this type-level confidence that some exceptions are not overlooked is an easy goal to meet and, once met, offers some (very) basic reassurance about the completeness of the code.

Practices that might work in the small, however, are under no obligation to scale. Java's checked exceptions were an experiment in combining control flow with types, and experiments produce results. The designers of C# learned from the experience (*https://oreil.ly/rCT18*):

> C# neither requires nor allows such exception specifications. Examination of small programs leads to the conclusion that requiring exception specifications could both enhance developer productivity and enhance code quality, but experience with large software projects suggests a different result—decreased productivity and little or no increase in code quality.

The designers of C#, of other JVM languages, of other non-JVM languages… whatever the original intent, the day-to-day reality of checked exceptions is they're perceived as obstacles. And if there's one thing programmers are skilled at, it's working around obstacles.

Compiler complaining about an unhandled checked exception? One IDE shortcut later, the obstacle is gone! In its place, you have an ever-lengthening `throws` clause that pushes incidental information into published signatures, often leaking details that should be encapsulated.

Or perhaps you add `throws Exception` or `throws OurCompanyException` to every method, noisily defeating the goal of being specific about failure?

How about catch-and-kill? If you're in a rush to push your code, there's nothing an empty `catch` block can't fix! You are Gandalf to the checked exception's Balrog—"You shall not pass!"

Checked exceptions bring and inspire syntactic baggage. But the issues run deeper. This is not simply a matter of programmer discipline or tolerating verbosity: for frameworks and extensible code, checked exceptions are flawed from the outset.

When publishing an interface, you're committing to a contract signed with method signatures. As Tolstoy recognized in *Anna Karenina*, the rainy-day scenarios are not as simple, as certain, or as knowable up front as the happy-day scenarios:

> All happy families are alike; each unhappy family is unhappy in its own way.

Interface stability is hard. Interface evolution is hard. Adding `throws` makes everything harder.

If someone plugs code into yours, and uses your code in their application, they know what they might be throwing, but you neither know nor care. Your code should let exceptions pass from their plugged-in code through to the handlers in their main application code. Open inversion of control demands exception transparency.

If they're using checked exceptions, however, they can't use your interfaces unless you add `throws Exception` to every method—noise that creates a burden on all dependent code—or unless they tunnel their exceptions wrapped in a `RuntimeException`...or unless they change their approach, standardizing on unchecked exceptions instead.

This last option is the lightest, most stable, and most open approach of all.

Unlocking the Hidden Potential of Integration Testing Using Containers

Kevin Wittek

Most Java developers have probably encountered the testing pyramid at one point in their career, whether as part of a computer science curriculum or mentioned in conference talks, articles, or blog posts. We can find a multitude of origin stories and variations of this metaphor (with a deep dive into those worthy of an article on its own) but, in general, it boils down to having a sizeable foundation of unit tests, followed by a smaller chunk of integration tests on top of that, and an even smaller tip of end-to-end UI tests.

This shape is proposed as an ideally optimal ratio of the different test classes. However, as with everything in software and computers, these guidelines need to be assessed in context, which means assuming integration tests to be slow and brittle. And this assumption is probably true if integration tests are expected to be run in a shared testing environment or require an extensive setup of local dependencies. But would the ideal shape still be a pyramid if we challenge these assumptions?

With ever more powerful machines, we can either use virtual machines (VMs) to wholly contain the complete development environment or use them to manage and run the external dependencies necessary for integration testing (such as databases or message brokers). But since most VM implementations aren't overhead free, this will add considerable load and resource consumption to the developer workstation. Also, start and creation times of VMs are too high for an ad hoc setup of a required environment as part of test execution.

The advent of user-friendly container technology, on the other hand, allows new testing paradigms to emerge. These low-overhead container implementations (being essentially an isolated process with its own self-contained file system) enable the creation and instrumentation of required services on demand and the usage of uniform tooling. Still, this instrumentation has been mostly done manually and laboriously outside of the actual test execution, slowing onboarding of new developers and introducing the potential for clerical mistakes.

In my opinion, the goal we as a community should strive for is to make the setup and instrumentation of the test environment an integral part of the test execution and even of the test code itself. In the case of Java, this means that executing a JUnit test suite, whether done by the IDE or the build tool, would implicitly lead to the creation and configuration of a set of containers necessary for the tests. And this goal is achievable with today's technology!

We can interact directly with the container engine using existing APIs or command-line tools, thereby writing our own "container driver"—note, however, the distinction between starting a container and the readiness of the service inside the container for testing. Alternatively, there is also the opportunity to explore the Java ecosystem for existing projects that deliver these functionalities on a higher level of abstraction. Either way, it's time to unleash the power of good integration tests and to emancipate them from the shackles of their past!

The Unreasonable Effectiveness of Fuzz Testing

Nat Pryce

Whether using test-driven development or not, programmers writing auto-mated tests suffer from positive test bias:[1, 2] they are more likely to test that the software behaves correctly when given valid input than that the software is robust when given invalid input. As a result, our test suites fail to detect entire classes of defects. *Fuzz testing*[3] is an unreasonably effective technique for negative testing that is easy to include in existing automated test suites. Including fuzz tests in your test-driven development process will help you build more robust systems.

For example, we were extending the software of a widely used consumer product to fetch data from web services. Although we were careful to write robust networking code and test-drove negative as well as positive cases, fuzzing immediately uncovered a surprising number of inputs that would make the software throw unexpected exceptions. Many of the standard Java APIs that parse data throw unchecked exceptions, so the type checker hadn't been able to ensure that the application handled all possible parsing errors. These unexpected exceptions could leave the device in an unknown state. In

1 Adnan Causevic, Rakesh Shukla, Sasikumar Punnekkat, and Daniel Sundmark, "Effects of Nega-tive Testing on TDD: An Industrial Experiment." In Hubert Baumeister and Barbara Weber, eds., *Agile Processes in Software Engineering and Extreme Programming: 14th International Conference*, XP 2013, Vienna, Austria, June 3–7, 2013. (Berlin: Springer, 2013), 91–105, *https://oreil.ly/qX_4n*.

2 Laura Marie Leventhal, Barbee M. Teasley, Diane S. Rohlman, and Keith Instone, "Positive Test Bias in Software Testing among Professionals: A Review." In Leonard.J. Bass, Juri Gornostaev, and Claus Unger, eds., *Human-Computer Interaction EWHCI 1993 Lecture Notes in Computer Science*, vol 753. (Berlin: Springer, 1993), 210–218, *https://oreil.ly/FTecF*.

3 Michael Sutton, Adam Greene, and Pedram Amini, *Fuzzing: Brute Force Vulnerability Discovery* (Upper Saddle River, NJ: Addison-Wesley Professional, 2007).

a consumer device, even one that can be updated remotely, that can mean an expensive increase in customer support calls or engineer callouts.

A fuzz test generates many random inputs, feeds them into the software under test, and checks that the software continues to exhibit acceptable behavior. To provide useful coverage, a fuzzer must generate inputs that are valid enough not to be rejected by the software immediately, but invalid enough to uncover corner cases that are not covered or defects in error-handling logic.

There are two ways to approach this:

- *Mutation-based fuzzers* mutate examples of good input to create possibly invalid test inputs.
- *Generation-based fuzzers* generate inputs from a formal model, such as a grammar, that defines the structure of valid inputs.

Mutation-based fuzzers are considered impractical for black box testing because it is difficult to obtain enough samples of valid input.[4] However, when we test-drive our code, the positive test cases provide a ready-made collection of valid inputs that exercise many of the control paths in the software. Mutation-based fuzzing becomes not just practical, but easy to apply.

Running thousands of random inputs through the entire system can take a long time. Again, if we fuzz during development, we can fuzz test particular functions of our system and design them so they can be tested in isolation. We then use fuzzing to check the correct behavior of those units and type checking to ensure that they compose correctly with the rest of the system.

Here's an example fuzz test that, along with the type checker, ensures a JSON message parser will throw only the checked exceptions declared in its signature:

```
@Test public void
only_throws_declared_exceptions_on_unexpected_json() {
    JsonMutator mutator = new JsonMutator();
    mutator.mutate(validJsonMessages(), 1000)
        .forEach(possiblyInvalidJsonMessage -> {
            try {
                // we don't care about the parsed result in this test
```

---

4 Charlie Miller and Zachary N.J. Peterson, "Analysis of Mutation and Generation-Based Fuzzing" (DefCon 15, 2007), 1–7.

```
      parseJsonMessage(possiblyInvalidJsonMessage);
    }
    catch (FormatException e) {
      // allowed
    }
    catch (RuntimeException t) {
      fail("unexpected exception: " + t +
          " for input: " + possiblyInvalidJsonMessage);
    }
  });
}
```

Fuzz testing is now an essential part of my test-driven development toolbox. It helps eliminate defects and guides the design of the system to be more compositional.

A simple library for doing mutation-based fuzz testing in Java and Kotlin projects is available on GitHub (*https://oreil.ly/nxVuC*).

Use Coverage to Improve Your Unit Tests

Emily Bache

Measuring the coverage of your tests is easier than ever. In a modern IDE, the button to run your tests with coverage is right next to the ones to run or debug them. The coverage results are presented class by class with little chart graphics, as well as relevant lines being highlighted in color in the source code.

Coverage data is easy to get hold of. What is the best way to use it, though?

When You're Writing New Code

Most people agree that you should deliver unit tests together with all the code you write. You can argue about which order to do things in, but in my experience, what works best is short feedback loops. Write a little test code, write a little production code, and build up the functionality together with the tests. When I'm working like this, I will run the tests with coverage from time to time as additional insurance that I haven't forgotten to test some new code I've just written.

The main danger here is that you become very satisfied with a high coverage number and don't notice you're missing both code and tests for a crucial piece of functionality. Perhaps you forgot to add error handling. Perhaps you missed out on a business rule. If you never wrote the production code in the first place, then coverage measurements can't discover that for you.

When You Have to Change Code You Didn't Write

Modifying code that you didn't write yourself that has poor or missing tests can be challenging—particularly if you don't really understand what it does but you still have to change it. When I'm faced with this situation, test coverage is one of the ways I learn about how good the tests are and which parts I can refactor more confidently.

I can also lean on the coverage data to discover new test cases and increase the covered areas. This can get dangerous, though. If I write tests purely to increase coverage, I can end up coupling the tests quite closely to the implementation.

When You're Working in a Team

One of the characteristics of a team is that you have "norms" or accepted behaviors that everyone agrees on, whether implicitly or explicitly. One of your team norms could be that you make coverage measurements part of your code and test review process. It can help you to see where tests are missing—perhaps some team members need more support and training to write better tests. It can also be encouraging when you see that complicated new functionality is well covered.

If you regularly measure test coverage for your whole codebase, I would encourage you to look at trends more than absolute numbers. I've seen arbitrary coverage targets lead to people preferring to test only what's easy to test. People can avoid doing refactoring because it will introduce new lines of code and lower their coverage overall. I've seen tests written with missing or very weak assertions just to improve the coverage numbers.

Coverage is supposed to help you improve your unit tests, and unit tests are supposed to make it easier to refactor. Coverage measurements are a tool to help you improve your unit tests and make your life easier.

Use Custom Identity
Annotations Liberally

Mark Richards

Annotations in Java are easy to write, easy to use, and very powerful—at least, some are. Traditionally, annotations in Java have provided a convenient way to implement aspect-oriented programming (AOP), a technique intended to separate out common behavioral concerns by injecting behavior at specified points in the code. However, most developers have largely abandoned AOP due to undesirable side effects as well as the desire to have all the code in one place—the class file.

Identity annotations are entirely different in that they don't contain any functionality. Instead, they only provide programmatic information that can be used to govern, analyze, or document some aspect of the code or architecture. You can use identity annotations to identify transaction boundaries or a domain or subdomain, describe a service taxonomy, denote framework code, and employ them in dozens of other use cases.

For example, identifying classes that are part of the underlying framework (or template code in microservices) is often important so changes can be closely monitored or guarded. The following annotation does just this:

```
@Retention(RetentionPolicy.RUNTIME)
@Target(ElementType.TYPE)
public @interface Framework {}

@Framework
public class Logger {...}
```

Wait—this annotation does nothing! Or does it? It denotes this class as a framework-related class, meaning changes to this class can impact almost all other classes. You can write automated tests to send a notification if any framework code has changed this iteration. It also lets developers know they are modifying a class that is part of the underlying framework code.

The following is a list of other common identity annotations I use on a regular basis (all of these are specified at the class level):

`public @interface ServiceEntrypoint {}`
> Identifies the entry point of a microservice. It's also used as a placeholder for other service description annotations listed below.
> Usage: `@ServiceEntrypoint`

`public @interface Saga {public Transaction[] value()...}`
> Identifies services that are involved in a distributed transaction. The `Transaction` value lists the transactions that span multiple services. It's added to classes that contain an `@ServiceEntrypoint` annotation.
> Usage: `@Saga({Transaction.CANCEL_ORDER})`

`public @interface ServiceDomain {public Domain value()...}`
> Identifies the logical domain (e.g., Payment, Shipping, Issuer, etc.) that the service belongs to (identified by the `Domain` value). It's added to classes that contain an `@ServiceEntrypoint` annotation.
> Usage: `@ServiceDomain(Domain.PAYMENT)`

`public @interface ServiceType {public Type value()...}`
> Identifies the classification of a service. The `Type` value enumerates the defined service types (classification). It's added to classes that contain an `@ServiceEntrypoint` annotation.
> Usage: `@ServiceType(Type.ORCHESTRATION)`

`public @interface SharedService {}`
> Identifies a class as one that contains common (shared) code across the application (e.g., formatters, calculators, logging, security, etc.).
> Usage: `@SharedService`

Identity annotations are a form of *programmatic documentation*. Unlike unstructured class comments, identity annotations provide a consistent means to ensure compliance or perform analytics, or they can be used to inform a developer of the context of a class or service. For example, you can leverage annotations when writing fitness functions using ArchUnit (*https://www.archunit.org*) to ensure all shared classes reside in the services layer of the application:

```
@Test
public void shared_services_should_reside_in_services_layer() {
    classes().that().areAnnotatedWith(SharedService.class)
    .should().resideInAPackage("..services..").check(myClasses);
}
```

Instead of comments, consider embracing identity annotations. Use them liberally to gain information, analytics, and programmatic control over your services or applications.

Use Testing to Develop Better Software Faster

Marit van Dijk

Testing your code will help you verify that your code does what you expect it to do. Tests will also help you to add, change, or remove functionality without breaking anything. But testing can have additional benefits.

Merely thinking about *what to test* will help to identify different ways the software will be used, discover things that are not clear yet, and better understand what the code should (and shouldn't) do. Thinking about *how to test* these things before even starting your implementation could also improve your application's testability and architecture. All of this will help you build a better solution before the tests and code are written.

Alongside the architecture of your system, think not only about what to test but also *where to test*. Business logic should be tested as close as possible to where it lives: unit tests to test small units (methods and classes), integration tests to test the integration between different components, contract tests to prevent breaking your API, etc.

Consider how to interact with your application in the context of a test, and use tools designed for that particular layer, from unit test (e.g., JUnit, TestNG), to API (e.g., Postman, REST-assured, RestTemplate), to UI (e.g., Selenium, Cypress).

Keep the goal of a particular test type in mind, and use the tools for that purpose, such as Gatling or JMeter for performance tests, Spring Cloud Contract testing or Pact for contract testing, and PITest for mutation testing.

But it is not enough to just use those tools: they should be used as intended. You could take a hammer to a screw, but both the wood and the screw will be worse off.

Test automation is part of your system and will need to be maintained alongside production code. Make sure those tests add value, and consider the cost of running and maintaining them.

Tests should be reliable and increase confidence. If a test is flaky, either fix it or delete it. Don't ignore it—you'll waste time later wondering why that test is being ignored. Delete tests (and code) that are no longer valuable.

A failing test should tell you *exactly* what is wrong *quickly*, without you having to spend a lot of time analyzing the failure. This means:

- Each test should test one thing.

- Use meaningful, descriptive names. Don't just describe what the test does either (we can read the code); tell us *why* it does this. This can help decide whether a test should be updated inline with changed functionality or whether an actual failure that should be fixed has been found.

- Matcher libraries, such as Hamcrest, can help provide detailed information about the difference between expected and actual results.

- Never trust a test you haven't seen fail.

Not everything can (or should) be automated. No tool can tell you what it's actually like to use your application. Don't be afraid to fire up your application and explore; humans are way better at noticing things that are slightly "off" than machines. And besides, not everything will be worth the effort of automating.

Testing should give you the right feedback at the right time to provide enough confidence to take the next step in your software development life cycle, from committing to merging to deploying and unlocking features. Doing this well will help you deliver better software faster.

Using Object-Oriented Principles in Test Code

Angie Jones

When writing test code, it's important to exercise the same care that you'd use when developing production code. Here are common ways to use object-oriented (OO) principles when implementing test code.

Encapsulation

The Page Object Model design pattern (*https://oreil.ly/guEVi*) is commonly used in test automation. This pattern prescribes creating a class to interact with a page of the application under test. Within this class are the locator objects for the elements of the web page and the methods to interact with those elements.

It's best to properly encapsulate by restricting access to the locators themselves and only exposing their corresponding methods:

```java
public class SearchPage {
    private WebDriver driver;
    private By searchButton = By.id("searchButton");
    private By queryField = By.id("query");

    public SearchPage(WebDriver driver){
        this.driver = driver;
    }

    public void search(String query) {
        driver.findElement(queryField).sendKeys(query);
        driver.findElement(searchButton).click();
    }
}
```

Inheritance

While inheritance should not be abused, it can certainly be useful in test code. For example, given there are header and footer components that exist on every page, it's redundant to create fields and methods for interacting with these components within every Page Object class. Instead, create a base Page class containing the common members that exist on every page, and have your Page Object classes inherit from this class. Your test code will now have access to anything in the header and footer no matter what Page Object they are currently interacting with.

Another good use case for inheritance within test code is when a given page has various implementations. For example, your app may contain a User Profile page that has different functionality based on roles (e.g., Administrator, Member). While there are differences, there could also be overlap. Duplicating code across two classes is not ideal. Instead, create a ProfilePage class that contains the common elements/interactions, and create subclasses (e.g., AdminProfilePage, MemberProfilePage) that implement the unique interactions and inherit the common ones.

Polymorphism

Assume we have a convenience method that goes to the User Profile page. This method doesn't know what type of profile page it is—an Administrator or a Member.

You're faced with a design decision here. Do you make two methods—one for each of the profile types? This seems like overkill since they both would do the exact same thing but just have a different return type.

Instead, return the superclass (ProfilePage) since both AdminProfilePage and MemberProfilePage are both subclasses of ProfilePage. The test method that is calling this convenience method has more context and can cast accordingly:

```
@Test
public void badge_exists_on_admin_profile() {
    var adminProfile = (AdminProfilePage)page.goToProfile("@admin");

    ...
}
```

Abstraction

Abstraction is used sparingly in test code, but there are valid use cases. Consider a type of widget that has been customized for different usages throughout the app. Creating an abstract class that specifies the behaviors expected is helpful when developing classes that interact with specific implementations of that widget:

```
public abstract class ListWidget {
    protected abstract List<WebElement> getItems();
    int getNumberOfItems() {
        return getItems().size();
    }
}


public class ProductList extends ListWidget {
    private By productLocator = By.cssSelector(".product-item");
    @Override
    protected List<WebElement> getItems() {
        return driver.findElements(productLocator);
    }
}
```

Test code is indeed code, meaning that it has to be maintained, enhanced, and scaled. Therefore, it's in your best interest to follow good programming practices when developing it—including the foundational OO principles.

Using the Power of Community to Enhance Your Career

Sam Hepburn

It's no longer enough to just be a great Java developer. If you want to advance your career, you need to be blogging, speaking at conferences, engaging on social media, committing to open source, and the list goes on. This can feel like a daunting task and you're probably asking yourself, "Why? Why is my technical ability not enough?" Well, the short answer is that a lot of the time, the people making decisions about your career will never see your code. You need to ensure that those people are hearing and seeing your name.

The Silver Lining

You don't need to do it *all*, and there are communities to help you along the way. If the idea of standing on a stage in front of 10, 50, 100, or more people literally puts you into a panic attack, don't do it.

On the other hand, if you're nervous and feel like you've got nothing to say, that's something that a community can help with. Have you ever fixed an issue you've been fighting with and thought to yourself, "If only I could have learned from someone who's done this already"? Everyone has these thoughts; they make for great subjects to cover in a talk or blog post.

If it's the fear of talking on stage, then start off small: present something to your team before submitting to a local Java User Group (JUG) or conference.

How Can Community Help?

As well as building your profile, another reason why engaging in community is so valuable is the content shared and conversations had. Technology is moving so fast that being a part of a community means you don't need to wait for a book to be published to get access to great content. The people writing those books, researching the latest technologies, are sharing their insights at community events, on blogs, and discussing them on forums.

The people in the communities that you're likely already involved with can all help you become better. From the speakers to the attendees, the things you learn from each other are sometimes more valuable than the overarching content of the event. Don't be afraid to ask questions of everyone in the room. Thought leadership can be shared in so many ways, and the people sitting next to you may have the answers you've been looking for.

If you're from a location that does not have a thriving Java community, don't panic—check out the Virtual JUG (*https://virtualjug.com*).

Looking for Your Next Challenge?

If you're after a new challenge, then community can really help you in your job search. If a hiring manager can avoid looking through the hundred applications on their desk to hire someone they know will fit in the team with the right skills, they'll do it.

What's the best way to get to the top of the pile? Find ways to interact outside of the application process. Meeting in person at local user groups will also allow you to understand what it's really like to work with the team. None of this candy-coated interview process only to find out on your first day that you're not in an environment that's right for you.

This circles back to where we started: the people making decisions about your career don't always see your code!

What Is the JCP Program and How to Participate

Heather VanCura

The Java Community Process (JCP) Program (*https://oreil.ly/t6agC*) is the process by which the international Java community standardizes and ratifies the specifications (*https://oreil.ly/vzEzX*) for Java technologies. The JCP Program ensures high-quality specifications are developed using an inclusive, consensus-based approach. Specifications ratified by the JCP Program must be accompanied by a Reference Implementation (to prove the Specification can be implemented) and a Technology Compatibility Kit (a suite of tests, tools, and documentation used to test implementations for compliance with the Specification).

Experience has shown that the best way to produce a technology specification is to use an open and inclusive process to develop a specification and implementation, informed by a group of industry experts with a variety of viewpoints. This also includes giving the community opportunities to review and comment, and also a strong technical lead to ensure the technical goals are met and the specification integrates with other relevant specifications.

An Executive Committee (EC) (*https://oreil.ly/J7Sng*) representing a cross-section of major stakeholders—such as Java vendors, large financial institutions utilizing Java to run their business, open source groups, and other members of the Java community, including individuals and user groups—is responsible for approving the passage of Specifications through the JCP Program's various stages and for reconciling discrepancies between Specifications and their associated test suites.

After being introduced in 1999, the JCP Program has continued to evolve over time using the process itself, through an effort called JCP.next, with the work being carried out in the open by the JCP EC. (*https://oreil.ly/8Xg8c*) JCP.next is a series of Java Specification Requests (JSRs) designed to focus on transparency, streamlining the JCP program, and broadening its membership. These JSRs modify the JCP's processes by modifying the JCP Process

Document. Once the changes are complete, they apply to all new JSRs and to future Maintenance Releases of existing JSRs for the Java platform.

For example, JSR 364 (*https://oreil.ly/q3X1U*), *Broadening JCP Membership*, was put into effect as JCP version 2.10. This JSR broadened JCP participation by defining new membership classes, enabling greater participation by the community, and helping ensure the appropriate intellectual property commitments from JCP Members. Any Java developer can join the JCP Program, and depending on the type of membership, JCP Members can participate as a JSR Spec Lead, Expert Group Member, or Contributor.

JSR 387 (*https://oreil.ly/ce2ag*), *Streamline the JCP Program*, was put into effect as version 2.11. This JSR streamlines the JSR life cycle process to bring it in line with the way Java technology is developed today, specifically enabling JSRs to be able to complete and keep up with the six-month Java platform release cycle cadence. Through this JSR we also resized the JCP EC.

With many changes in the Java community, the continuation of the JCP Program remains constant. Anyone can apply to join (*https://oreil.ly/eSzdV*) and participate in the JCP Program—either as a Corporation or Non-Profit (Full Member), Java User Group (Partner Member), or Individual (Associate Member). The stability of the JCP Program and participation from community members (*https://oreil.ly/z8rot*) ensures continued success of the Java platform and its future. Standards enable execution of technical strategies, and the JCP enables collaboration of industry and participation from the developer community.

Compatibility matters—the Spec, RI, and TCK required by the JCP Program enable an ecosystem to be built up around Java technologies. The JCP Program provides the foundation and structure for this—IP rights and obligations are covered, and choice in implementations that pass the TCK benefits the ecosystem—this is key to success and continued popularity of Java technology.

Why I Don't Hold Any Value in Certifications

Colin Vipurs

Some time back—it must have been around the mid-noughties—one of my friends had taken and passed the Java Certified Programmer exam with an impressive score of 98%. Eager to keep up, I took one of the practice tests during a lunch break and, although I didn't score as high, I got a passing grade. One question on the exam has always stuck in my mind. It was to do with the inheritance hierarchy in Swing applications, something I had no problem answering as my day job was working with Swing, but it did strike me as odd to ask something that could easily be looked up in your IDE. I never did get around to taking the exam, mostly due to being partway through studying for my master's degree at the time.

Fast-forward a few years, and I had just started a new job. During the first week, I was asked by one of my new colleagues if I was Java 5 certified. "No," I replied, "but I have been using it for the last year." Turns out he was certified, so good news for me that someone on my team would have a base level of knowledge and skill. It was less than two weeks later that he asked why we have to bother overriding `hashCode` when we override `equals`. He genuinely didn't understand the relationship between the two methods. This was just the tip of what he didn't know, yet he was certified!

Fast-forward another few years, and I'm contracting at a place where the company policy was that every permanent employee be certified, at least to what was then the Java Certified Programmer level. I did meet some good developers there, and good developers had passed through the ranks, but there were some truly awful developers as well—all of whom were certified.

A quick look at the Oracle site for Java Certification tells you that being certified will "Help you position yourself with validation that you posses the full skill set and knowledge to be a Professional Java Developer" and "Earn you more credibility, help you perform better in your daily job, and lead your team and company forward." Rubbish. Being a "professional developer" and performing "better in your day job" have little to do with what you'll need in order to become certified. You can learn enough to pass the exams without ever writing a line of code. As an industry, we can't even definitively tell you what "good" and "bad" are, so a piece of paper claiming to do so is worthless.

There are, of course, exceptions to every rule. I have met a few people—well, at least one—who have used Java certification as a way to bolster their own knowledge. They used it as a way to learn things they otherwise wouldn't have had to as part of their day job, and to those people I take my hat off. In over twenty years of writing software professionally, one thing about certifications has never changed: the good developers don't need it, but the bad ones can easily achieve it.

Write One-Sentence Documentation Comments

Peter Hilton

> *A common fallacy is to assume authors of incomprehensible code will somehow be able to express themselves lucidly and clearly in comments.*
>   —Kevlin Henney

You're probably either writing too many comments in your code, or none at all. Too many generally means too many to maintain, which risk becoming dangerously inaccurate comments that you're better off deleting. Too many is also likely to mean that they're badly written and unimproved, because it's hard to write "lucidly and clearly." None at all means relying on perfect naming, code structure, and tests, which is even harder than it sounds.

We've all seen a lot of code whose authors didn't write any comments at all, whether to save time, because they didn't want to, or because they thought their code was self-documenting. Sometimes code really is that well written: the first thousand lines of a new project, the hobby project written in artisanal handcrafted code, and maybe the mature well-maintained library project whose narrow focus keeps the codebase small.

Large applications are different, especially enterprise business applications. Comments are a problem when you're maintaining 100,000 lines of code that other people wrote and are still adding to. That code isn't all going to be perfect, and needs some explanation. The hard question is how much explanation: how many comments?

The answer to commenting large application codebases is to write one-sentence documentation comments, as follows:

1. Write the best code you can.

2. Write a one-sentence documentation comment for every public class and method/function.

3. Refactor the code.

4. Delete unnecessary comments.

5. Rewrite bad comments (because all good writing requires rewriting).

6. Only add detail where absolutely necessary.

This approach helps you discover which comments are necessary, either because the code cannot explain things like why it exists or because you haven't had time to refactor it yet. You find out when you write the one-sentence comment: if a good comment takes several minutes to write, then it's necessary and will save you and other readers time in the future.

If you wrote a good comment as fast as you can type, then you identified "obvious" code that doesn't need the comment, which you must immediately delete. The trick is that this discovery requires actually writing the comment, however obvious you think the code is, and especially if you wrote it yourself. Do not skip this step!

You always need a minimum number of comments that *comment only what the code cannot say*,[1] answering the *why* questions that you can't answer in code. Limiting these to one sentence per public interface makes the writing, code review, and maintenance effort realistic, and lets you focus on quality and brevity.

Don't write more than one sentence unless you really have to. There might be more *why* questions, unusual complexity, or obscure domain language jargon to explain, especially abbreviations. Delegate where you can: problem domains often have Wikipedia pages you can link to.

Comments are amazingly useful if they're good, mainly because we spend more time reading code than writing it. Comments are also the only feature common to all general programming languages. When programming, use the best language for the job. Sometimes, it's English.

---

1 *97 Things Every Programmer Should Know* (O'Reilly)

Write "Readable Code"

Dave Farley

We have all heard that good code is "readable," but what does that really mean?

The first principle of readability is to keep the code simple. Avoid lengthy methods and functions; instead, break them into smaller pieces. Name the pieces for what they do.

Automate your coding standards so you can test them in your deployment pipeline. For example, you could fail your build if you have a method of more than 20 to 30 lines of code, or parameter lists of more than 5 or 6 parameters.

Another way toward better readability is to take "readable" literally. Don't interpret it as meaning "Can I read my code five minutes after I wrote it?" Rather, try to write code that a nonprogrammer could understand.

Here is a simple function:

```
void function(X x, String a, double b, double c) {
    double r = method1(a, b);
    x.function1(a, r);
}
```

What does it do? Without looking into the implementation of X and method1, you have no way of telling, programmer or not.

But if instead I wrote this:

```
void displayPercentage(Display display, String message,
                       double value, double percentage) {
  double result = calculatePercentage(value, percentage);
  display.show(message, result);
}
```

it would be clear what was going on. Even a nonprogrammer could probably guess from the names what is happening here. Some things are still hidden—

we don't know how the display works or how the percentage is calculated—but that is a good thing. We can understand what this code is attempting to do.

For simple examples like this, this kind of change looks too trivial to discuss, but how much of the code you see at work looks like this?

Taking naming seriously, combined with simple refactoring techniques, allows you to quickly gain deeper insight into what is happening in your code.

Here is another example, in this case from some real-world code:

```
if (unlikely(!ci)) {
    // 361 lines of code
} else {
    // 45 lines of 'else'
}
```

Highlight the unlikely(!ci) and create a new method called noConnection.

Highlight the 361 lines in the if statement and name it createConnection, and you end up with:

```
if (noConnection(ci)) {
    ci = createConnection();
} else {
    // 45 line of 'else'
}
```

Naming things sensibly, even if that means pulling out a function that is only used once in order to name it, creates clarity in code that is missing otherwise. It will also often highlight the fact that there are significant opportunities to simplify the code. In this example, there were five other places in the same file that could have reused the new createConnection method. I would take this further and rename ci to connection or something more appropriate.

Because we have improved the code's modularity, this approach also gives us more options for further change. For example, we could now decide to hide some more of the complexity in this method and simply use the connection, whether created here for the first time or not:

```
ci = createConnection(ci);
// 45 lines of code
```

Make functions and methods simple. Make all names meaningful in the context of the problem you are solving: functions, methods, variables, parameters, constants, fields, anything!

Imagine your nontechnical grandpa or grandma reading the code: could they guess at what it was doing? If not, make the code simpler through refactoring, and more expressive through the selection of good names.

The Young, the Old, and the Garbage

María Arias de Reyna

One of the major advantages of Java is that developers have not had to worry (much) about memory. In contrast to many other languages around at the time of its launch, Java has, since the beginning, freed unused memory automatically. But that doesn't mean Java developers don't need to know the basics of how Java handles memory. There can still be memory leaks and bottlenecks.

Java divides its memory into two segments:

Heap	Instances, variables…your data
Nonheap/perm	Code, metadata…for the JVM

To care about memory in Java, we should focus on the heap. It is divided into two generations depending on their lifetime: young and old. The *young generation* (aka the *nursery*) contains short-lived objects. The *old generation* contains structures that have survived longer.

The young generation is divided in two:

Eden	Where objects are created
Survivor	An in-between, limbo state through which an instance will pass when moving from the *young* to the *old* space

The Garbage Collector

The garbage collector (GC) is the system cleaning the memory. There are different implementations, but in general it performs two tasks:

Minor collection	Reviews the young generation
Major collection	Reviews all memory, young and old

The GC runs at the same time as the normal app execution. Each execution of the GC involves a pause (usually milliseconds) in all running threads. While your application remains healthy, the GC usually limits its actions to minor collections as not to interfere with it.

GC Strategies

For proper operation and cleaning of memory, we should have small, short-lived objects rather than objects that live a long time. The temporary objects will stay in Eden, so the GC will remove them earlier and faster.

Having unused objects in memory doesn't disrupt the execution of your app, but it may affect your hardware performance. It may also slow down the GC execution, as it will process them over and over again on each execution.

It may seem tempting to force a GC execution calling `System.gc`. However, this will force a major collection, disrupting heuristics and stopping your application while this collection lasts.

References

The GC frees instances that are no longer referenced, meaning if you create an instance with an attribute referencing a second instance, both instances will be either removed at the same time or never. The more cross-referenced instances, the more complex and error-prone the GC task is. You can help the GC by nulling attributes on objects to break links between instances.

All static objects live forever. This means all their referenced attributes will also live forever.

To help the GC collect unwanted objects, there are special types of references whose corresponding classes can be found in `java.lang.ref`:

Weak reference | Does not count as a reference for cleanup. For example, we can use `WeakHashMap` (*https://oreil.ly/6PGRj*), which works as a `HashMap` (*https://oreil.ly/B_6ss*), but using weak references. So, if the map contains an object that is only referenced in the map, it can be removed.

Soft reference | The GC respects the link and removes the instance, depending on demand for memory.

Phantom reference | Always returns `null`. The link doesn't really point to the object. Used to clear instances before taking the object that binds it.

Remember that the garbage collector is your friend. It tries to make your life easier. You can return the favor by making its job easier too.

Contributors

Abraham Marin-Perez

 Abraham Marin-Perez is a Java programmer, consultant, author, and public speaker with over 10 years of experience in industries ranging from finance to publishing to the public sector. After graduating in computer science at the University of Valencia, Spain, Abraham relocated to London to work at J.P. Morgan, while also getting a BSc in telecommunications. After three years in finance, he switched to online betting for another three years, and then became an independent contractor. Abraham benefited greatly from the London programming community, and decided to give back and share his experience by becoming a Java news editor at InfoQ, speaking at conferences like Devoxx or CodeOne (née JavaOne), authoring *Real-World Maintainable Software* (O'Reilly), and coauthoring *Continuous Delivery in Java* (O'Reilly). Always the learner, Abraham is currently studying for a degree in physics. He also helps run the London Java Community and provides career advice at the Meet a Mentor group.

The Code Restorer, page 28

Adam Bien

 Adam Bien (*adambien.blog*) is a developer, consultant, author, podcaster, and Java enthusiast. He's been using Java since JDK 1.0 and JavaScript since LiveScript and still enjoys writing code. Adam regularly organizes Java EE, WebStandards, and JavaScript workshops at Munich airport (*airhacks.com*) and runs a monthly Q&A live streaming show at *airhacks.tv*.

Follow the Boring Standards, page 53

Alexey Soshin

Alexey Soshin is a software architect with 15 years of experi-
ence in the industry. He is the author of the book *Hands-On
Design Patterns with Kotlin* (Packt Publishing) and the *Web
Development with Kotlin* video course. Alexey is a Kotlin and
Vert.x enthusiast and an experienced conference speaker.

CountDownLatch—Friend or Foe?, page 32

A.Mahdy AbdelAziz

A.Mahdy AbdelAziz is a technical trainer and a public
speaker. He has more than 12 years of experience in the
software field, including Google, Oracle, and three start-ups.
A.Mahdy cofounded @ExtraVerd and is interested in modern
technologies such as PWA, offline-first design, machine
learning, and the cloud stack. If he is not talking in front of a microphone or
sitting in an airplane, you can find him playing basketball. Reach him on
Twitter as @__amahdy or GitHub as *@amahdy*.

Events Between Java Components, page 47

Anders Norås

Originally educated in arts and design, Anders has spent the
last 20 years writing code. He currently works for Itera as
chief technology officer. He has given numerous talks and
keynotes at conferences such as JavaZone, NDC, J-Fall,
Øredev, and many more. He has given 100-plus conference
talks to a variety of audiences including media, design, and hardcore computer science. He is known for his energetic and highly engaging presenta-
tions. This is his second feature for the *97 Things* series.

All You Need Is Java, page 1

Angie Jones

Angie Jones is a senior developer advocate who specializes
in test automation strategies and techniques. She shares her
wealth of knowledge by speaking and teaching at software
conferences all over the world, writing tutorials and technical
articles on *angiejones.tech*, and leading the online learning
platform, Test Automation University. As a Master Inventor, Angie is

known for her innovative and out-of-the-box thinking style, which has resulted in more than 25 patented inventions in the US and China. In her spare time, Angie volunteers with Black Girls Code to teach coding workshops to young girls in an effort to attract more women and minorities to tech.

Using Object-Oriented Principles in Test Code, page 196

Ben Evans

Ben Evans is principal engineer and architect for JVM technologies at New Relic. Prior to joining New Relic, Ben cofounded jClarity (acquired by Microsoft) and was chief architect (Listed Derivatives) at Deutsche Bank. Ben is the author of *The Well-Grounded Java Developer* (Manning Publications), *Java: The Legend* (O'Reilly), *Optimizing Java* (O'Reilly), and the recent editions of *Java in a Nutshell* (O'Reilly). He is the track lead for Java/JVM at InfoQ, writes regularly for industry publications, and is a frequent speaker at technical conferences worldwide. Ben has been active in free and open source software for over 20 years, cofounded the AdoptOpenJDK initiative (with Martijn Verburg), and served on the JCP Executive Committee for six years.

Java Is a '90s Kid, page 84
Java's Unspeakable Types, page 90

Benjamin Muschko

Benjamin Muschko is a software engineer and a consultant and trainer with over 15 years of experience in the industry. He's passionate about project automation, testing, and Continuous Delivery. Ben is a frequent speaker at conferences and is an avid open source advocate. Software projects sometimes feel like climbing a mountain. In his free time, Ben loves hiking Colorado's 14ers and enjoys conquering long-distance trails.

"But It Works on My Machine!", page 23

Benjamin Muskalla

Benjamin Muskalla ("Benny," *@bmuskalla*) for the past 12 years has been following his passion of building tools for improving developer productivity. He has been an active committer of the world-class Eclipse IDE. Over the years, he's spent a lot of time building tools, frameworks, and test approaches to help his peers become more effective. TDD and API design are dear to his heart as well as working on open source software. Benny currently works for Gradle Inc. on the Gradle Build Tool.

Refactoring Toward Speed-Reading, page 155

Billy Korando

Billy Korando is a developer advocate with IBM with more than a decade of experience. Billy is passionate about helping developers find ways to reduce mental capacity waste from tedious work, such as project initiation, deployment, testing and validation, and so on through automation and good management practices. Outside of work, Billy enjoys traveling, playing kickball, and cheering on the Kansas City Chiefs. Billy also co-organizes the Kansas City Java Users Group.

Improving Repeatability and Auditability with Continuous Delivery, page 72

Brian Vermeer

Brian Vermeer is a developer advocate for Snyk and a software engineer with over 10 years of hands-on experience in creating and maintaining software. He is passionate about Java, (pure) functional programming, and cybersecurity. Brian is an Oracle Groundbreaker Ambassador, Utrecht JUG co-lead, Virtual JUG organizer, and co-lead at MyDevSecOps. He is a regular international speaker on mostly Java-related conferences like JavaOne, Devoxx, Devnexus, Jfokus, JavaZone, and many more. Besides all that, Brian is a military reserve for the Royal Netherlands Air Force and a Taekwondo Master/Teacher.

Take Good Care of Your Dependencies, page 162

Burk Hufnagel

Burk Hufnagel is a programmer and solution architect with Daugherty Business Solutions, where he's focused on finding ways to deliver better code, faster, and teaching others how to do the same. He's on the board of directors for the Atlanta Java User Group and helps run the Devnexus conference. He's presented at user group meetings and technical conferences including Connect.Tech, Devnexus, JavaOne, and Oracle Code One. In 2010, Burk was recognized as a JavaOne Rock Star. As a writer, Burk contributed multiple articles to *97 Things Every Software Architect Should Know* and *97 Things Every Programmer Should Know* (O'Reilly). He's also served as a technical reviewer for several books, including *Head First Software Development* (O'Reilly) and Kathy Sierra and Bert Bates's *Sun Certified Programmer for Java Study Guide* (McGraw-Hill), for which he received an unexpected compliment: "Burk fixed more of our code than we care to admit."

Deliver Better Software, Faster, page 36

Carlos Obregón

Carlos Obregón has been working in software development since 2008. Because he has always had a passion for sharing knowledge, he started a Java User Group in Bogotá, now called Bogotá JVM, where he has given talks primarily on best practices in the Java language. Besides developing software, he coordinates bootcamps related to topics about web development. He first started dating C++ but, before graduating from university, he found true love with Java. After some years, he tried dating other JVM languages but found that no other language gave him as much joy as Java. Besides coding, he also loves spending time with family and friends playing board games and video games. He also tries to read at least a book per month, mainly technical books but also literature. Nothing is more important to him than Lina, Mariajosé, and Evie—his wife, daughter, and dog.

How to Avoid Null, page 67

Chris O'Dell

Chris O'Dell has spent nearly 15 years as a backend engineer, primarily with Microsoft technologies, but recently with Go on a large microservices platform. She has led teams delivering highly available web APIs, distributed systems, and cloud-based services. She has also led teams developing internal build and deployment tooling with the goal of improving the developer's experience. Chris currently works at Monzo helping to build the future of banking. Chris is a regular conference speaker on the topics of Continuous Delivery and development practices. She is a contributor to the book *Build Quality In* (Leanpub) and coauthored the book *Continuous Delivery with Windows and .NET* (O'Reilly).

Frequent Releases Reduce Risk, page 55

Christin Gorman

Christin Gorman has been writing software professionally for 20 years and has gained experience in everything from start-ups to large enterprises, always hands-on, writing code. She is best known for her enthusiastic public speaking style and for blogging about software. A common underlying theme of hers is the importance of developers being involved in the software they are creating. Software developers are tragically underutilized—relegated to picking isolated tasks from a board someone else has set up, writing code in styles, languages, and frameworks they had no say in choosing, and never once getting to meet the users of their software. Christin is passionate about getting developers more involved, unleashing their potential, and making them care about every aspect of what they are working on, not just so they have more fun at work but more importantly so the products they create are more useful. Christin currently works for the Norwegian consultancy Kodemaker.

Do You Know What Time It Is?, page 38

Colin Vipurs

Colin Vipurs just celebrated his twenty-first anniversary as a developer. He's been around a lot in the UK, worked in finance, press, music, and aeronautics, and currently works at Masabi, in the public transit space. Back in the day he used to do a lot of C/Perl, then moved to Java, dabbled in Scala for a bit, and now does mostly full-time Kotlin. He wrote a book once and does conference speaking when he can be bothered to put some material together. His passions are TDD/BDD, building scalable, high performance systems, and food.

Why I Don't Hold Any Value in Certifications, page 203

Daniel Bryant

Daniel Bryant works as a product architect at Datawire, and is the news manager at InfoQ and chair for QCon London. His current technical expertise focuses on "DevOps" tooling, cloud/container platforms, and microservice implementations. Daniel is a Java Champion and leader within the London Java Community (LJC). He also contributes to several open source projects, writes for well-known technical websites such as InfoQ, O'Reilly, and DZone, and regularly presents at international conferences such as QCon, JavaOne, and Devoxx.

The Benefits of Codifying and Asserting Architectural Quality, page 14
The Case Against Fat JARs, page 26

Daniel Hinojosa

Daniel Hinojosa is a programmer, consultant, instructor, speaker, and author. With over 20 years of experience, he does work for private, educational, and government institutions. Daniel loves JVM languages like Java, Groovy, and Scala, but also works with non-JVM languages like Haskell, Ruby, Python, LISP, C, and C++. He is an avid Pomodoro Technique practitioner and makes every attempt to learn a new programming language every year. Daniel is the author of *Testing in Scala* (O'Reilly) and the video of the *Beginning Scala Programming* video series for O'Reilly Media. For downtime, he enjoys reading, swimming, Legos, football, and cooking.

Know Thy flatMap, page 98

Dave Farley

Dave Farley is a thought leader in the field of Continuous Delivery. He is coauthor of the Jolt-award winning book *Continuous Delivery* (Addison-Wesley), a regular conference speaker and blogger, one of the authors of the Reactive Manifesto, and a contributor to the thinking behind BDD. Dave has been having fun with computers for over 35 years and has worked on most types of software, firmware, commercial applications, and low-latency trading systems. He started working in large-scale distributed systems more than 30 years ago, researching the development of loose-coupled, message-based systems—a forerunner of microservices. Dave is a former director of innovation at ThoughtWorks and head of software development at LMAX Ltd., home of the OSS Disruptor, a company well known for the excellence of their code and the exemplary nature of its development process. Dave is now an independent consultant, and founder and director of Continuous Delivery Ltd.

Take "Separation of Concerns" Seriously, page 164
Test-Driven Development, page 168
Write "Readable Code", page 207

David Delabassee

David Delabassee has been involved in the Java ecosystem for more than two decades. He lives and breathes Java! These days he works as a developer advocate in the Java Platform Group at Oracle. Over the years, he has championed Java extensively throughout the world by presenting at conferences and user groups. David has authored numerous technical articles and trainings, and he occasionally blogs at *delabassee.com*. In his spare time, he is actively involved in multiple nonprofit organizations focused on improving rights for individuals with disabilities. He is also an accessibility activist. David lives in Belgium, where he enjoys playing video games with Lylou, his lovely (but challenging to beat) daughter.

Be Aware of Your Container Surroundings, page 7

Dawn and David Griffiths

 Dawn and David Griffiths are the authors of *Head First Kotlin* and *Head First Android Development* (O'Reilly). They have also written other books in the *Head First* series and developed the animated video course *The Agile Sketchpad* as a way of teaching key concepts and techniques in a way that keeps your brain active and engaged.

Thinking in Coroutines, page 174

Dean Wampler

 Dean Wampler (*@deanwampler*) is an expert in streaming systems, focusing on ML/AI. He is head of developer relations at Anyscale.io, which is developing Ray for distributed Python. Previously, he was an engineering VP at Lightbend, where he led the development of Lightbend Cloudflow, an integrated system for streaming data applications with popular open source tools. Dean has written books for O'Reilly and contributed to several open source projects. He is a frequent conference speaker and tutorial teacher, and a co-organizer of several conferences and user groups in Chicago. Dean has a PhD in physics from the University of Washington.

Embrace SQL Thinking, page 45

Donald Raab

 Donald Raab has more than 18 years of experience as a software engineer in the financial services industry. He started programming with Java in 1997 and has programmed in 20-plus programming languages over the years. He is a member of the JSR 335 Expert Group and is also the creator of the Eclipse Collections Java Library that was originally open sourced as GS Collections in 2012 and migrated to the Eclipse Foundation in 2015. Donald was selected as a 2018 Java Champion, and he is a frequent speaker and guest trainer at key Java conferences and user group meetups including Oracle CodeOne, JavaOne, QCon New York, Devnexus, Devoxx US, EclipseCon, JVM Language Summit, and Great Indian Developer Summit (GIDS).

Learn to Kata and Kata to Learn, page 108

Edson Yanaga

Edson Yanaga, Red Hat's director of developer experience, is a Java Champion and a Microsoft MVP. He is also a published author and a frequent speaker at international conferences, discussing Java, microservices, cloud computing, DevOps, and software craftsmanship. Yanaga considers himself a software *craftsman*, and is convinced that we all can create a better world for people with better software. His life's purpose is to deliver and help developers worldwide to deliver better software faster and safely—and he can even call that a job!

Behavior Is "Easy"; State Is Hard, page 9

Emily Bache

Emily Bache is a technical agile coach with ProAgile. She helps teams to improve the way they write code together, and teaches test-driven development. Emily lives in Gothenburg, Sweden, but is originally from the UK. She is the author of *The Coding Dojo Handbook* (self-published) and often speaks at international conferences.

Approval Testing, page 3
Use Coverage to Improve Your Unit Tests, page 189

Emily Jiang

Emily Jiang is a Java Champion (*https://oreil.ly/HheKg*). She is also a Liberty Microservices Architect and Advocate, senior technical staff member (STSM) for IBM, based at Hursley Lab in the UK. Emily is a MicroProfile guru and has been working on MicroProfile since 2016. She leads the specifications of MicroProfile Config, Fault Tolerance, and Service Mesh. She is also a CDI Expert Group member. Emily is passionate about Java, MicroProfile, and Jakarta EE. She regularly speaks at conferences such as QCon, Code One, Devoxx, Devnexus, JAX, Voxxed, EclipseCon, GeeCON, JFokus, and more. You can find her on Twitter *@emilyfhjiang* and LinkedIn (*http://www.linkedin.com/in/emily-jiang-60803812*).

Make Code Simple and Readable, page 120

Gail C. Anderson

Gail C. Anderson is a Java Champion, Oracle Groundbreaker Ambassador, and past member of the NetBeans Dream Team. She is director of research and founding member of the Anderson Software Group, a leading provider of training courses in Java, JavaFX, Python, Go, Modern C++, and other programming languages. Gail enjoys researching and writing about leading-edge Java technologies. Her current passion includes JavaFX with GraalVM for cross-platform mobile applications. She is the coauthor of eight textbooks on software programming. Most recently, she is a contributing author to *The Definitive Guide to Modern Java Clients with JavaFX: Cross-Platform Mobile and Cloud Development* (Apress). Gail has presented at various Java conferences and JUGS including Devoxx, Devnexus, JCrete, and Oracle Code/JavaOne worldwide. Twitter: *@gail_asgteach*. Website: *asgteach.com*.

Learn to Use New Java Features, page 113

Dr. Gail Ollis

Dr. Gail Ollis has been programming ever since she learned BASIC on the school's one computer in the math storeroom. Many programming languages later, her career has spanned professional software development, research into the psychology of software development, and lecturing to undergraduate and master's students on programming and cyberpsychology. The continuous thread throughout this is her passion to help people do programming better across a wide range of experience, from tutoring in computer science and coaching early career developers, to conducting industry-relevant academic research to develop practical support for cybersecurity in professional software development.

Don't hIDE Your Tools, page 40

Heather VanCura

Heather VanCura is the director and chairperson of the Java Community Process (JCP) program. In her role she is responsible for leadership of the community. She also serves as an international speaker, mentor, and leader of hack days. VanCura oversees the work of the JCP Executive Committee, the *JCP.org* website, JSR management, community building,

---

Contributors

events, communications, and growth of the membership. She is also a contributor and leader of the community-driven user group adoption programs. She is the spec lead for JSRs as part of the ongoing JCP.Next effort to evolve the JCP program itself. Heather is based in the Bay Area of California, is passionate about Java and developer communities, and enjoys trying new sports and fitness activities in her free time. You can find her on Twitter: *@heathervc*.

What Is the JCP Program and How to Participate, page 201

Dr. Heinz M. Kabutz

Dr. Heinz M. Kabutz is the author of the mildly entertaining and somewhat useful #Java Specialists' Newsletter, which can be found at *javaspecialists.eu*. He can be reached via email at *heinz@javaspecialists.eu*.

Read OpenJDK Daily, page 145

Holly Cummins

Holly Cummins is an IBMer and leads the developer community in the IBM Garage. As part of the Garage, Holly uses technology to enable innovation for clients across a range of industries, from banking to catering to retail to NGOs. She has led projects to count fish using AI, help a blind athlete run ultramarathons in the desert solo, improve health care for the elderly, and change how city parking works. Holly is also an Oracle Java Champion, IBM Q Ambassador, and JavaOne Rock Star. Before joining the IBM Garage, she was delivery lead for the WebSphere Liberty Profile (now Open Liberty). Holly coauthored Manning's *Enterprise OSGi in Action* and is still happy to explain why OSGi is great. Before joining IBM, Holly completed a DPhil in quantum computation. Holly is organized with her woolly scarves, and hasn't lost one yet—but she regularly loses her winter coat (brrr).

Garbage Collection Is Your Friend, page 61
Java Should Feel Fun, page 88

Ian F. Darwin

 Ian F. Darwin has worked in the computer field for ages, on systems of almost every size, shape, and OS. He codes in multiple languages including Java, Python, Dart/Flutter, and shell scripting, and has made open source contributions to OpenBSD, Linux, and other projects. He's worked at Toronto's University Health Network, where he built the first Android version of Medly, a lifesaving mHealth app. Best known for the *Java Cookbook* and the *Android Cookbook* (O'Reilly), he's written and taught Unix and Java courses for Learning Tree, and an undergrad course on Unix and C for the University of Toronto. Ian also writes on travel, electric cars, medieval literature, and any other "smoother pebble or prettier shell than ordinary" that he trips over at the seashore. Find him at *darwinsys.com* or on Twitter as *@Ian_Darwin*.

Think Outside the Java Sandbox, page 172

Ixchel Ruiz

 Ixchel Ruiz has developed software applications and tools since 2000. Her research interests include Java, dynamic languages, client-side technologies, and testing. She is a Java Champion, Groundbreaker Ambassador, Hackergarten enthusiast, open source advocate, JUG leader, public speaker, and mentor.

Build Diverse Teams, page 19

James Elliot

 James Elliott is a senior software engineer at Singlewire in Madison, Wisconsin, with 30 years professional experience as a systems developer. Loving everything from 6502 assembler through Java, he's delighted to find himself working in Clojure today, both at work and in his open source side projects as Deep Symmetry, occasionally DJing, and producing electronic music shows with his partner, Chris. James has written and coauthored several books and updated editions for O'Reilly and enjoys mentoring new generations of developers in the ever-changing (yet fundamentally timeless) world of software.

Augment Javadoc with AsciiDoc, page 5
Rediscover the JVM Through Clojure, page 151

Jannah Patchay

Jannah Patchay is an industry-recognized subject matter expert and consultant in the financial markets sector, specializing in financial markets innovation and in helping firms define, develop, and execute their commercial strategies in a highly regulated environment. Her particular passion is for market structure—the participants in financial markets, how they interact, and the consequences of the ways in which they interact—and for finding creative solutions to the challenges around access to markets and liquidity. This encompasses both traditional financial markets and asset classes, and the emerging field of digital asset markets. Jannah is also a director and regulatory advocacy ambassador for the London Blockchain Foundation, and she writes on financial and technology innovation topics for *Best Execution* magazine. Jannah has a BSc in mathematics and computer science from the University of Cape Town, and an LLM in international banking and finance law from the University of Liverpool.

The Three Traits of Really, Really Good Developers, page 178

Jeanne Boyarsky

Jeanne Boyarsky is a Java Champion and lives in New York City. She has written five books about Java certification. Jeanne has been paid to do Java for 17 years. She volunteers at *coderanch.com* and with a FIRST robotics team. Jeanne regularly speaks at conferences and is a Distinguished Toastmaster, which involves giving over 50 speeches.

Break Problems and Tasks into Small Chunks, page 17
It's Done, But..., page 80
Learn Java Idioms and Cache in Your Brain, page 106

Jenn Strater

Jenn Strater is a longtime Groovy community member and manager of the Groovy Community slack. She has contributed to various open source projects including CodeNarc, Gradle, Groovy, and Spring REST Docs. As a conference speaker, Jenn has presented at events such as Devoxx Belgium, the Grace Hopper Celebration of Women in Computing, SpringOne Platform, and the O'Reilly Velocity Conference. In 2013, she founded the organization GR8Ladies (now GR8DI) through which she mentors students and junior developers. She is a graduate of Hamilton College in Clinton, NY, and was a Fulbright grant recipient in 2016-2017. She currently resides in the Twin Cities.

Builds Don't Have To Be Slow and Unreliable, page 21
Only Build the Parts That Change and Reuse the Rest, page 132
Open Source Projects Aren't Magic, page 134

Jennifer Reif

Jennifer Reif is an avid developer and problem-solver. She has contributed to projects for both developer communities and large enterprises to organize and make sense of widespread data assets and leverage them for maximum value. She has worked with a variety of commercial and open source tools and enjoys learning new technologies, sometimes on a daily basis! Learning and writing code are core parts of her daily activities, and she enjoys creating content to share with others. Frequently, her content includes speaking at conferences and developer-focused events, as well as writing. Her passions are finding ways to organize chaos and delivering software more effectively. Other passions include her cats, traveling with family, hiking, reading, baking, and horseback riding.

In the Language Wars, Java Holds Its Own, page 74

Jessica Kerr

Jessica Kerr is a symmathecist, in the medium of code. She believes in learning systems made of learning parts: enthusiastic people and evolving software. In 20 years of professional software development, she has worked in languages from Java to Scala and Clojure, from Ruby to Elixir and Elm, from Bash to TypeScript and PowerShell. In her years as a conference keynoter and speaker, she has talked about all of these, plus the deeper work of software development. She finds inspiration in resilience engineering, systems thinking, and art. She loves helping developers automate the boring bits of our work and express more creativity in the rest. Find her learning out loud on Twitter (*@jessitron*), live coding on Twitch (jessitronica), writing at *blog.jessitron.com*, and raising two new unpredictable people in her home in St. Louis, MO.

From Puzzles to Products, page 57

Josh Long

Josh Long (*@starbuxman*) is an engineer with decades of experience writing code. He's also the first Spring Developer Advocate, a Java Champion, an author of books (including O'Reilly's *Cloud Native Java: Designing Resilient Systems with Spring Boot, Spring Cloud, and Cloud Foundry* and the self-published *Reactive Spring*) and numerous best-selling video trainings (including *Building Microservices with Spring Boot Livelessons* with Spring Boot cocreator Phil Webb). Josh is a frequent face at conferences, having spoken in hundreds of cities around the world, on every continent (except Antarctica). Josh loves to write code. He's an open source contributor (Spring Framework, Spring Boot, Spring Integration, Spring Cloud, Activiti, Vaadin, MyBatis, etc.), a podcaster (*A Bootiful Podcast*) and a YouTuber (*Spring Tips* (*http://bit.ly/spring-tips-playlist*)).

Production Is the Happiest Place on Earth, page 141

Ken Kousen

Ken Kousen is a Java Champion, Oracle Groundbreaker Ambassador, Java RockStar, and Grails Rock Star. He is the author of the O'Reilly books *Kotlin Cookbook*, *Modern Java Recipes*, and *Gradle Recipes for Android*, and the Manning book *Making Java Groovy*, as well as several video courses on the O'Reilly Learning Platform. He is a regular presenter on the No Fluff Just Stuff conference tour, and has spoken at conferences all over the world. Through his company, Kousen IT, Inc., he has taught software development to thousands of students and working professionals.

Make Your Java Groovier, page 122

Kenny Bastani

Kenny Bastani is a passionate technology evangelist and an open source software advocate in Silicon Valley. As an enterprise software consultant, he has applied a diverse set of skills needed for projects requiring a full-stack web developer in Agile mode. As a passionate blogger and open source contributor, Kenny engages a community of passionate developers who are looking to take advantage of newer graph processing techniques to analyze data.

Trade-Offs in a Microservices Architecture, page 180

Kevin Wittek

 Kevin Wittek is a Testcontainers co-maintainer and a Testcontainers-Spock author who is passionate about FLOSS and Linux. He received the Oracle Groundbreaker Ambassador award for his contributions to the open source community. Kevin is a Software Craftsman and testing fan. He fell in love with TDD because of Spock. Kevin believes in Extreme Programming as one of the best Agile methodologies. He likes to write MATLAB programs to support his wife in performing behavioral science experiments with pigeons. Kevin plays the electric guitar and is a musician in his second life. After many years working in the industry as an engineer, Kevin is now doing his PhD at RWTH Aachen on the topic of verification of Smart Contracts and is leading the Blockchain Research Lab at the Institute for Internet Security in Gelsenkirchen at the Westphalian University of Applied Sciences.

Kevlin Henney

 Kevlin Henney (@*KevlinHenney*) is an independent consultant, trainer, coder, and writer. His development interests are in programming, languages, and practice, helping individuals, teams, and organizations to get better at these. He has a deep love of programming and languages, which he is delighted to have found has also worked out as a profession for over three decades. Kevlin has given keynotes, tutorials, and workshops at hundreds of conferences and meetups around the world. He has been a columnist for various magazines, journals, and websites, a contributor to open and closed-source software, and a member of more groups, organizations, and committees than is probably healthy (it has been said that "a committee is a cul-de-sac down which ideas are lured and then quietly strangled"). He is coauthor of *A Pattern Language for Distributed Computing* and *On Patterns and Pattern Languages*, two volumes in the *Pattern-Oriented Software Architecture* series (Wiley), and editor of *97 Things Every Programmer Should Know* (O'Reilly).

Kirk Pepperdine

Kirk Pepperdine has been performance-tuning Java applications for more than 20 years. He is the author of the original Java Performance Tuning Workshop. In 2006, Kirk was named a Java Champion for his thought leadership in the Java performance space. He speaks frequently at user groups and conferences and has been named a JavaOne Rockstar numerous times. Kirk continues to be an ardent supporter of the Java community as the cofounder of JCrete, a Java unconference that has been used as a template for a number of other unconferences in Europe, Asia, and North America. In 2019 Kirk's start-up, jClarity, was acquired by Microsoft, where he is now employed as a principal engineer.

Hey Fred, Can You Pass Me the HashMap?, page 65

Liz Keogh

Liz Keogh is a Lean and Agile consultant based in London. She is a well-known blogger and international speaker, a core member of the BDD community, and a passionate advocate of the Cynefin framework and its ability to change mindsets. She has a strong technical background with 20 years of experience in delivering value and coaching others to deliver, from small start-ups to global enterprises. Most of her work now focuses on Lean, Agile, and organizational transformations, and the use of transparency, positive language, well-formed outcomes, and safe-to-fail experiments in making change innovative, easy, and fun.

Feedback Loops, page 49

Maciej Walkowiak

Maciej Walkowiak is an independent software consultant. He helps companies take architectural decisions as well as designing and developing systems based primarily on Spring stack. An active Spring community member, he has been a contributor to several Spring projects. In recent years, he has become more and more passionate about teaching and sharing knowledge. Maciej runs a YouTube channel (Spring Academy), speaks at conferences, and spends too much time on Twitter.

"Full-Stack Developer" Is a Mindset, page 59

Mala Gupta

Mala Gupta is a developer advocate at JetBrains and founder and lead mentor at *eJavaGuru.com*, coaching Java Certifications aspirants to succeed. A Java Champion, she promotes learning and usage of the Java technologies at various platforms through her Java books, courses, lectures, and speaking engagements. She is a firm believer in the equality of responsibilities and opportunities for all. She has over 19 years of experience in the software industry as an author, speaker, mentor, consultant, technology leader, and developer. As an author with Manning Publications, her Java titles books are top-rated for Oracle Certification around the globe. A frequent speaker at industry conferences, she co-leads the Java User Group-Delhi chapter. A strong supporter of Women in Technology, she drives initiatives of Women Who Code, Delhi Chapter, to augment the participation of women in tech.

Java Certifications: Touchstone in Technology, page 82

Marco Beelen

Marco Beelen is a software crafter, with a passion for maintainable and readable code. Marco has been working as a software developer since 2005. Prior to that Marco was a system administrator, which instilled in him the importance of observability of software systems. Marco has been the host of various Code Retreats and meetups, including a miniseries on test-driven development. Marco is married and the father of two children. He prefers "Drink your own champagne" over "Eat your own dog food" (especially since he likes to drink champagne). He can be found online as *@mcbeelen*.

Package-by-Feature with the Default Access Modifier, page 139

María Arias de Reyna

María Arias de Reyna is a Java senior software engineer, geospatial enthusiast, and open source advocate. She has been a community leader and core maintainer of several free and open source projects since 2004. María is currently working at Red Hat, where she focuses on Middleware and maintains Apache Camel and Syndesis. She is an experienced keynoter and speaker. Between 2017 and 2019, María was the elected president of OSGeo, the Open

Source Geospatial Foundation, which serves as an umbrella for many of the most relevant geospatial software. She is also a feminist and a Women In Technology activist.

The Young, the Old, and the Garbage, page 210

Mario Fusco

Mario Fusco is a principal software engineer at Red Hat, working as Drools project lead. He has huge experience as a Java developer, having been involved in (and often leading) many enterprise-level projects in several industries ranging from media companies to the financial sector. His interests include functional programming and Domain-Specific Languages. By leveraging these two passions, he created the open source library lambdaj with the purposes of providing an internal Java DSL for manipulating collections and allowing a bit of functional programming in Java. He is also a Java Champion, the JUG Milano coordinator, a frequent speaker, and the coauthor of *Modern Java in Action* published by Manning.

Concurrency on the JVM, page 30
Let's Make a Contract: The Art of Designing a Java API, page 118

Marit van Dijk

Marit van Dijk has almost 20 years of experience in software development in different roles and companies. She loves building awesome software with amazing people, and is an open source core contributor to Cucumber, as well as an incidental contributor to other projects. She enjoys learning new things, as well as sharing knowledge on programming, test automation, Cucumber/BDD, and software engineering. She speaks at international conferences, in webinars, and on podcasts, and blogs at *medium.com/ @mlvandijk*. Marit is currently employed as a software engineer at *bol.com*.

Use Testing to Develop Better Software Faster, page 194

Mark Richards

Mark Richards is an experienced, hands-on software architect involved in the architecture, design, and implementation of microservices architectures, event-driven architectures, and distributed systems. He has been in the software industry since 1983 and has a master's degree in computer science. Mark is the founder of *DeveloperToArchitect.com*, a free website devoted to helping developers in the journey to software architect. He is also an author and conference speaker, having spoken at hundreds of conferences worldwide and written numerous books and videos on microservices and software architecture, including his latest book, *Fundamentals of Software Architecture* (O'Reilly).

Use Custom Identity Annotations Liberally, page 191

Michael Hunger

Michael Hunger has been passionate about software development for more than 35 years, 25 of which have been within the Java ecosystem. For the last 10 years, he has been working on the open source Neo4j graph database, filling many roles, most recently leading the Neo4j Labs efforts. As caretaker of the Neo4j community and ecosystem, he especially loves to work with graph-related projects, users, and contributors. As a developer, Michael enjoys many aspects of programming languages, learning new things every day, participating in exciting and ambitious open source projects, and contributing to and writing software-related books and articles. Michael has helped organize conferences and has spoken at many more. His efforts got him accepted to the Java Champions program. Michael helps kids learn to program by running weekly girls-only coding classes at local schools.

Benchmarking Is Hard—JMH Helps, page 11
Firing on All Engines, page 51

Mike Dunn

Mike Dunn is the principal mobile engineer and Android technical lead at O'Reilly Media. He is a recognized member of the AOSP community and a dedicated contributor to the Android open source ecosystem. He is the original creator of the popular and longstanding tiling image library, TileView. Mike is also the coauthor of *Native Mobile Development: A Cross-*

Reference for Android and iOS Native Development with Shaun Lewis (O'Reilly), and the upcoming *Programming Android with Kotlin: Java to Kotlin by Example* with Pierre-Olivier Laurence (O'Reilly). He's contributed to Google's Closure JavaScript library, and provided open source support ranging from color management libraries to fast-seeking, block-level encryption with Google's next-gen Android media player ExoPlayer, to a tightly compact PHP routing engine. Mike has been programming professionally for nearly 20 years, and is continuing to study computer science in the master's program at the Georgia Institute of Technology. You can find several levels of variously antiquated and aging-into-obsolescence code snippets, open source and client projects, as well as his blog, at Mike's home page (*http://moagrius.com*).

Kotlin Is a Thing, page 103

Monica Beckwith

Monica Beckwith is a Java Champion, First Lego League Coach, and coauthor of *Java Performance Companion* (Addison-Wesley). She is the sole author of the upcoming *Java 11 LTS+—A Performance Perspective*. She is passionate about JVM performance at Microsoft.

Java Programming from a JVM Performance Perspective, page 86

Nat Pryce

Nat Pryce has been programming for <coughty-cough> years, many of those using Java and/or the JVM. He has worked as consulting developer and architect in a variety of industries, and delivered business-critical systems that range in scale from embedded consumer devices to large compute farms supporting global business. He is a regular conference speaker and one of the authors of *Growing Object-Oriented Software, Guided by Tests* (Addison-Wesley), a popular book on object-oriented design and test-driven development.

The Unreasonable Effectiveness of Fuzz Testing, page 186

Nicolai Parlog

Nicolai Parlog (aka nipafx) is a Java Champion with a passion for learning and sharing. He does that in blog posts, articles, newsletters, and books; in tweets, repos, videos, and streams; at conferences and in-house trainings—more on all of that on *nipafx.dev*. That aside, he's best known for his haircut.

Kinds of Comments, page 96
Optional Is a Lawbreaking Monad but a Good Type, page 136
Take Care of Your Module Declarations, page 160

Nikhil Nanivadekar

Nikhil Nanivadekar is a committer and project lead for the open source Eclipse Collections framework. He has been working in the financial sector as a Java developer since 2012. Prior to starting his career as a software developer, Nikhil received his bachelor's degree in mechanical engineering from the University of Pune, India, and a master's degree in mechanical engineering with a specialization in robotics from the University of Utah. Nikhil was designated as a Java Champion in 2018. He is a regular on the local and international speaker circuit. He is also a strong advocate for children's education and mentorship, and hosts several workshops teaching robotics to kids at events like JCrete4Kids, JavaOne4Kids, OracleCodeOne4Kids, and Devoxx4Kids. Nikhil enjoys cooking with his family, hiking, skiing, motorcycle riding, and working with animal rescue and relief organizations.

Know Your Collections, page 101

Patricia Aas

Patricia Aas is an experienced C++ programmer who started off as a Java programmer. She has worked on two browsers, Opera and Vivaldi, and built embedded telepresence systems at Cisco. An extremely curious person, she's always excited to learn new things. Today she works as a consultant and trainer for TurtleSec, a company she cofounded, where she specializes in application security.

Inline Thinking, page 76

Paul W. Homer

Paul W. Homer has been a professional software developer for the last 30 years. He has built commercial products for finance, marketing, printing, and health care and has spent the last 15 years blogging about it. At some point or another, he's dabbled in just about every aspect of software development as well as often being the lead programmer. His blog *The Programmer's Paradox* is an attempt to synthesize some sanity from these diverse experiences. It discusses the larger patterns he's encountered while moving between different organizations. He prefers backend algorithmic coding but often takes pleasure in trying to make domain interfaces fully dynamic. When he is not buried in complex code, he tries to spend his time talking to developers and entrepreneurs about the foundations of software development.

The Necessity of Industrial-Strength Technologies, page 130

Peter Hilton

Peter Hilton is a product manager, developer, writer, speaker, trainer, and musician. His professional interests are product management, workflow automation, software functional design, Agile software development methods, and software maintainability and documentation. Peter consults for software companies and development teams, and delivers the occasional presentation and workshop. Peter has previously presented at numerous European developer conferences, and he coauthored the book *Play for Scala* (Manning Publications). He has taught Fast Track to Play with Scala and, more recently, his own training course, How to Write Maintainable Code.

Get Better at Naming Things, page 63
Refactor Boolean Values to Enumerations, page 153
Write One-Sentence Documentation Comments, page 205

Rafael Benevides

Rafael Benevides is a cloud native developer advocate at Oracle. With many years of experience in several fields of the IT industry, he helps developers and companies all over the world to be more effective in software development. Rafael considers himself a problem-solver who has a big love for sharing. He is a member of Apache DeltaSpike PMC, a Duke's Choice

Award project winner, and is a speaker at conferences like JavaOne, Devoxx, TDC, Devnexus, and many others. He is on Twitter as *@rafabene*.

Really Looking Under the Hood, page 147

Rod Hilton

Rod Hilton is a software engineer working with Scala and Java at Twitter. He blogs about software, technology, and sometimes *Star Wars* at *nomachetejuggling.com*. You can find him on Twitter as *@rodhilton*.

There Are Great Tools in Your bin/ Directory, page 170

Dr. Russel Winder

Dr. Russel Winder was first a theoretical high energy particle physicist and then retrained himself as a Unix systems programmer. This led to him becoming a computer science academic (University College London, then King's College London) interested in programming; programming languages, tools, and environments; concurrency; parallelism; build; human–computer interaction; and sociotechnical systems. Having been Professor of Computing Science and head of the department of computer science at King's College London, he left academia to dabble with start-ups as CTO or CEO. After this he was an independent consultant, analyst, author, trainer, and expert witness for a decade before retiring in 2016. He is still very interested in programming; programming languages, tools, and environments; concurrency; parallelism; and build—it keeps him active during retirement.

Declarative Expression Is the Path to Parallelism, page 34
The JVM Is a Multiparadigm Platform: Use This to Improve Your Programming, page 92
Threads Are Infrastructure; Treat Them as Such, page 176

Sam Hepburn

Sam Hepburn has spent the past nine years in London becoming a well-known face of the tech start-up scene. She has worked with a variety of organizations within London and now works further afield in the US, UK, and Poland, building some of the largest tech communities in the world. Her main aim is to create environments for individuals to feel welcome and for communities to flourish. She's currently leading the community team at Snyk.io helping developers adopt security into their development workflows. In her personal time, she is the cofounder of Circle, a network for advancing women's careers in our new world of work, and the host of *Busy Being Human*, a podcast covering the unedited, honest, human story behind how our favorite humans became who they are.

Using the Power of Community to Enhance Your Career, page 199

Sander Mak

Sander Mak is director of technology at Picnic, a Dutch online grocery scale-up, building Java-based systems at scale. He also is a Java Champion and author of the O'Reilly book *Java 9 Modularity*. As an avid conference speaker, blogger, and Pluralsight author, Sander loves sharing knowledge.

The Rebirth of Java, page 149

Sebastiano Poggi

Sebastiano Poggi, emerging from the foggy plains of northern Italy, cut his teeth working at an early days smartwatch start-up. He moved with his curls to London to help on big clients' Android apps at renowned agencies AKQA and Novoda. A Google Developer Expert since 2014, he frequently speaks at conferences and sporadically writes blog articles. Being back in Italy, these days he's working for JetBrains on both a tooling product and an Android app. He's got a knack for good design, typography, and photography, and has a past as a videomaker. Sebastiano can often be found expressing unrequested opinions on *twitter.com/seebrock3r*.

Interop with Kotlin, page 78

Steve Freeman

Steve Freeman, coauthor of *Growing Object-Oriented Software, Guided by Tests* (Addison-Wesley), was a pioneer of Agile software development in the UK. His experience includes working for consultancies and software vendors, as an independent consultant and trainer, and prototyping for major research laboratories. Steve has a PhD from Cambridge University. Currently, he is a distinguished consultant with Zuhlke Engineering Ltd., based in the UK. Steve's main pastime is trying not to buy any more trombones.

Don't Vary Your Variables, page 42
Minimal Constructors, page 125
Simple Value Objects, page 157

Thomas Ronzon

Thomas Ronzon has focused on the modernization of business-critical applications for more than 20 years. In addition, he publishes articles and speaks at conferences. Thomas dives passionately, gladly, and deeply into technical aspects, with professionalism. With empathy, experience, and concrete proposals for solutions, he helps build the bridge between business and IT.

How to Crash Your JVM, page 70

Trisha Gee

Trisha Gee has developed Java applications for a range of industries, including finance, manufacturing, software, and nonprofit, for companies of all sizes. She has expertise in Java high-performance systems and is passionate about enabling developer productivity. Trisha is a developer advocate for JetBrains, a leader of the Sevilla Java User Group, and a Java Champion. She believes healthy communities and sharing ideas help us to learn from mistakes and build on successes.

Keep Your Finger on the Pulse, page 94
Learn Your IDE to Reduce Cognitive Load, page 116
Technical Interviewing Is a Skill Worth Developing, page 166

Uberto Barbini

 Uberto Barbini is a polyglot programmer with more than 20 years of experience designing and building successful software products in many industries. He discovered that he loves programming when he created his first video game on the ZX Spectrum, and he is still very passionate about how to write the best code to deliver value to the business, not only once but at a regular pace. When not coding, Uberto loves public speaking, writing, and teaching. He's currently writing a book about pragmatic functional Kotlin.

Learn to Love Your Legacy Code, page 111

Index

A

abstractions, 34
  missing, 66
  using in test code, 198
acceptance tests, 49
access modifiers, 140
actor model, 30
Akka, 30
algorithms, 92
aliasing, 157
allocation size and rate, 87
analytics and data, using to test software, 50
Android, 78, 175
  using Kotlin in development, 103
annotations
  nullability, 78
  using custom identity annotations, 191
anticorruption layer, 10
Apache Groovy (see Groovy)
APIs
  designing, 118
  documentation with Javadoc, 5
application frameworks, 1
application servers, 53
approval testing, 3
architectural quality, benefits of codifying and asserting, 14

ArchUnit, 14, 192
arrange–act–assert (tests), 144
AsciiDoc
  benefits of, 5
  origin and evolution of, 6
aspect-oriented programming (AOP), 191
AsyncGetCallTrace, 52
auditability, improving with continuous delivery, 73
automated testing, 17, 194
autonomy, 142
@Autowired annotation, 127
availability, 180

B

backend developers, 59
backward compatibility, 58
Bazel, 132
  remote build caching, 133
benchmarking
  characterizing and validating benchmarks, 86
  difficulty of on JVM, 11
  measuring impact of presizing collections, 11
better software, 36
big data frameworks, 98
bin/ directory, 170

block comments, 97
boilerplate, 46, 88, 104, 158, 162
Boolean values, refactoring to enumerations, 153
browsers, backward compatibility of, 54
bugs in proportion to lines of code, 146
build tool runtime, standardized version of, 23
builds
    improving efficiency with build caching, 132
    reproducibility and maintainability wih standardized tools, 23
    running acceptance tests in, 49
    slow and unreliable, fixing, 21
business logic frameworks, 2
byte code instrumentation, 51
bytecode
    as target platform, languages making use of, 93
    saving bytes in early Java, 84
    verification in the JVM, disabling, 71

C

C, 173
C#, 182
caching, 76
    build caching, 132
CAP theorem, 180
certifications in Java, 82
    why I hold no value in, 203
character encodings, 147
checked exceptions, 182
CI/CD
    continuous delivery (CD), 141
    improving repeatability and auditability with continuous delivery, 72
    running wrappers on pipeline, 24
class files, modifying in the filesystem, 70
class libraries in Java, 1
classes

    naming, 64
    representing value objects, 157
    thinking carefully about responsibilities of, 164
    unnecessary, 45
Clojure, 173
    built-in software transactional memory, 31
    rediscovering the JVM through, 151
cloud-native applications, 147
code
    making simple and readable, 120
    reading OpenJDK daily, 145
    writing readable code, 207
code change vs. system change, 58
code katas, 108
code restorers, 29
collections
    importance of, 101
    presizing, measuring impact of, 11
command line, 40
comments, 96
    block comments, 97
    commenting code when necessary, 120
    in module declarations, 160
    Javadoc comments, 96
    line comments, 97
    using identity notations instead of, 192
    writing one sentence documentation comments, 205
commits, frequent, 17
common Java interview questions, 167
Communicating Sequential Processes (CSP), 177
communication and clarity, 80
community
    JCP, and how to participate, 201
    using to enhance your career, 199
compilation, build tool caching of, 132
compilers

U

ubiquitous vocabulatory, 63
unchecked exceptions, 183
underfitting tests, 144
undifferentiated heavy lifting, 142
unhandled checked exceptions, 182
unit of test (UoT), isolating, 87
unit testing frameworks
    JUnit, 3
    using with ArchUnit, 14
unit tests, 49
    good unit tests (GUTs), 143
    using coverage to improve, 189
    using with katas, 108
unknown unknowns, testing and, 56
unordered collections, 101
unreliable builds, 21
Unsafe class, 71
unsorted collections, 101

V

value objects, simple, 157
varargs, 119
variables
    local variables not marked as final in
        OpenJDK, 146

meaningful names for, 120
variables, not varying, 42
    assigning once, 42
    localizing scope, 43
verbose code, avoiding, 121
verbosity of Java, 75, 88, 122
vocabulary, development in writing pro-
    grams, 65
vulnerabilities in dependencies, 162

W

weak references, 211
web development technologies, 59
web/JavaScript ecosystem, lack of stand-
    ardization in frameworks, 53
Windows, running Maven Wrapper goals
    on, 24
WORA (write once, run anywhere) princi-
    ple, 74
wrappers, 23

Y

young generation, 210

Z

ZonedDateTime, 38

O'REILLY®

There's much more where this came from.

Experience books, videos, live online training courses, and more from O'Reilly and our 200+ partners—all in one place.

Learn more at oreilly.com/online-learning

Milton Keynes UK
Ingram Content Group UK Ltd.
UKHW021842190924
448478UK00009B/173